brita housez, long devoted to healthy cooking, has been cooking and baking daily with soy products for more than seven years. She is the author of *Tofu Mania* and lives in St. Catharines, Ontario, Canada.

the soy dessert and baking book

also by **brita housez**
tofu mania

brita housez

Add Soy—and Nutrition—
to Your Favorite Cakes,
Cookies, Pies, Tarts,
Muffins, Quick
Breads, Puddings,
and Other Desserts

the soy dessert and baking book

Photographs by Zeva Oelbaum
Food styling by Victoria Granof

marlowe & company
new york

THE SOY DESSERT AND BAKING BOOK:

Add Soy—and Nutrition—to Your Favorite Cakes, Cookies, Pies, Tarts, Muffins, Quick Breads, Puddings, and Other Desserts

Published by

Marlowe & Company

An Imprint of Avalon Publishing Group Incorporated

161 William Street, 16th Floor

New York, NY 10038

Library of Congress Cataloging-in-Publication Data

Housez, Brita.

    The soy dessert and baking book : add soy—and nutrition—to your favorite cakes, cookies, pies, tarts, muffins, quick breads, puddings, and other desserts / by Brita Housez.

       p. cm.

    ISBN 1-56924-589-4

    1. Cookery (Soybeans) 2. Desserts. 3.Soyfoods. I.Title.

TX803.S6 .H68 2001

641.8'6—dc21

2001044457

9 8 7 6 5 4 3 2 1

Designed by Pauline Neuwirth, Neuwirth and Associates, Inc.

Printed in the United States of America

Distributed by Publishers Group West

contents

cookies

squares & bars

cakes & frostings

pies & tarts

pancakes, crêpes, cobblers & dumplings

muffins, biscuits & quick breads

yeast breads

hot & cold puddings

custards, mousses, soufflés & trifles

creams & sauces

confections

beverages

introduction

IT'S TIME for dessert and you have a choice between two luscious-looking cakes that smell and taste incredibly good. There are, however, significant differences between these seemingly identical sweets. One is overflowing with calories and saturated fats, is made from processed ingredients that have been robbed of their essential nutrients, and probably contains harmful additives such as artificial colors and sweeteners. The other cake has reduced calories and fat (especially saturated fats) and consists of natural, cholesterol-free, good-for-you soy products along with other nutritious ingredients. Which cake will you choose?

The Soy Dessert and Baking Book makes it easier than ever to choose the more nutritious cake—in fact, to make a wide variety of desserts and baked goods using soy products.

I have been baking for many years—really almost all of my life. My grandmother was a devoted and very talented baker, as is my mother, and I learned the art and craft of baking from scratch from both of them. About five years ago, I began to experiment with using tofu and soy products in all of my cooking, as a way of feeding my family more nutritiously. I had read extensively about the health benefits of tofu and soy products and, in particular, about soy's ability to lower "bad" cholesterol. I became determined to develop recipes containing tofu and to include tofu in my daily cooking. My first cookbook, *Tofu Mania*, was a direct result of those efforts. But because I also love to bake, I realized that I could incorporate soy products into all of my baking. My own growing interest in cooking and baking with soy products coincided with the arrival on supermarket shelves with a wide variety of soy products. I set out to stock my refrigerator and pantry shelves with these products and to experiment incorporating them into my favorite recipes for desserts and baked goods. I am devoted to baking and this book now makes available the many recipes I've had the pleasure of developing.

the health benefits of soy

Soy originated in China and quickly spread to other Asian and European countries, where it has been valued for centuries as a nutritious source of vegetable protein. Plentiful and cheap, soy remains a common ingredient in most Asian dishes. In recent years, its health benefits have been recognized and documented in North America through scientific studies which confirm that soy can indeed help us live longer and healthier lives, provided we consume it in small amounts on a daily basis.

These studies have shown that a balanced diet that includes soy can help protect us from many debilitating diseases. Soybeans are the only vegetable food that contains complete protein as well as all eight amino acids required for good health. It is an excellent source of vitamin B, calcium, magnesium, and minerals, as well as dietary fiber. By simply adding soy foods to our diet, we can reduce the risk of certain types of cancer, such as breast, colon, prostate, stomach, uterine, and ovarian. Though there are many cancer-fighting substances found in soy, the isoflavone *genistein* has been proven to be the element that inhibits the growth of cancer cells, including some of the cells most resistant to treatment. Genistein is also a potent antioxidant that protects healthy cells from the effects of noxious free radicals.

In addition to its cancer-preventing qualities, there is evidence that incorporating soy into our diet can help prevent and treat heart disease. Soy isoflavones are able to block the formation of free radicals that damage arteries. They can also prevent blood clots, thereby reducing the risk of heart attack and stroke. Soy has been proven to significantly decrease high concentrations of cholesterol in the blood that, again, may lead to a decrease in the risk of coronary heart disease. The FDA has recognized soy's health benefits and given its official seal of approval, authorizing food manufacturers to claim that products containing at least 6.25 grams of soy protein per serving and are low in fats and cholesterol reduce the risk of coronary heart disease.

Another fantastic health benefit found in soy products is the presence of phytoestrogens (hormones that mimic estrogen in humans), which help relieve the uncomfortable symptoms of menopause. A recent study of post-menopausal women showed that eating soy on a daily basis reduced the occurrence and intensity of hot flashes and night sweats. Osteoporosis, or bone loss, is another major threat to post-menopausal women. Once women reach age thirty, their bones absorb less calcium, resulting in a decrease in bone density. The addition of calcium-rich soy to our diet may prevent or alleviate this crippling disorder.

•   •   •

what kind of soy products should you buy?

Due to the worldwide controversy over the safety of genetically engineered foods, I like to buy organic foods whenever possible. According to consumer advocates Ronnie Cummins and Ben Lilliston, authors of *Genetically Engineered Food*, there is increasing evidence that "genetically engineered foods may cause toxic effects, exposure to allergens and elevate cancer risks." In recent years, consumers have become better informed about the quality of the food they eat. This awareness has made them more health-conscious and has created a growing demand for organic foods which, as a result, are becoming more readily available, not only at health food stores but also at regular supermarkets and bulk stores. Several brands of soy foods now offer organic products made from non-genetically engineered soybeans. Just check the labels for confirmation.

Soy's popularity as a health food has prompted pharmaceutical companies to develop many different kinds of soy supplements. Although they may contain some essential nutrients, none of these supplements possess the isoflavones genistein and *dadzein*, the primary healing elements found in natural soy foods and an integral part of soy's amazing health benefits.

how to add soy to your desserts and baking without sacrificing great taste

Despite its newfound popularity in North America, the uses of soy remain a puzzle to many people. They may order a veggie burger at a fast food restaurant or buy ready-made tofu dips, spreads, or soy beverages at their local grocer, but aside from tossing the occasional tofu cube into soups and stir-fries and using soy milk in shakes, they are still hesitant to incorporate this "miracle food" into their cooking, let alone into desserts and baking! People wonder how a slice of cheesecake or a double chocolate chip cookie, made with soy ingredients, could possibly taste as good as the real thing. What they don't understand is that with so many different delicious soy products on the market today, it has become a snap to substitute them for more fattening and less healthy ingredients, without sacrificing taste.

In my last book, *Tofu Mania*, I incorporated tofu into recipes in such a way that one could hardly notice its presence in a dish. In *The Soy Dessert and Baking Book* I have strived to meet the same challenge: The result is a collection of dessert and baking recipes that incorporate an array of nutritious soy foods and other healthy ingredients without losing any of the delicious taste.

how much soy should we eat?

Throughout this book, I have greatly reduced the level of saturated fats found in the traditional version of these recipes by replacing a portion of them with a variety of cholesterol- and lactose-free soy foods such as tofu, soy cream cheese, soy sour cream, soybean oil, soy protein isolate, soy milk, and soy milk powder. Whenever possible, I have also replaced a portion of the egg yolks with these same soy foods.

The secret to maintaining the authentic flavor you love and expect when, for instance, you bite into a luscious slice of tiramisu, is to use soy only as a partial substitute for the ingredients you normally use, thereby allowing the soy to absorb their flavors. After all, there is no need to "overdose" on soy. In order to maximize soy's health benefits, doctors recommend ingesting only 25 to 40 grams (about 1 ounce) of soy each day. This translates into 1 cup (7 grams) of soy milk; 4 ounce (10 grams) of tofu; ¼ cup (17 grams) of soynuts; ¼ cup (8 grams) of soy flour.

treat your sweet tooth to a little soy throughout the day

Let me give you some examples of how easily you can begin—today!—to make soy an integral part of your diet. For breakfast, add extra protein and fiber to your cereal or pancakes, by making Fruit Flummery (page 147) or Blueberry Pancakes (page 88). Or perhaps you'd prefer something light, like the nutritious Protein Berry Shake (page 194). How about a slice of Pineapple Cranberry Loaf (page 120) as a mid-morning snack? Or hot-out-of-the-oven Quick 'N' Easy Carrot Scones (page 112). An after lunch dessert might be a serving of Strawberry Shortcake (page 100), Crème Caramel à l'Orange (page 158), or Ultra Light Cheesecake (page 47). With afternoon tea or coffee, tangy Lemon Squares (page 33) or moist Chocolate Brownies (page 20) sound inviting, or perhaps you're in the mood for a couple of soft Coconut Macaroons (page 11) or crisp Lemon Cookies (page 10). For a casual after dinner dessert, warm Apple Pie (page 64) or Sugar 'N' Spice Squares (page 29) sounds appealing while Cheesecake with Swirled Lemon Curd (page 48) or Raspberry Orange Trifle (page 167) are more appropriate for a festive occasion. Do you have a craving for a bite-sized late night treat? Chocolate Soynut Butter Truffles (page 185) or White Chocolate Cherry Bars (page 25) would certainly hit the spot.

All of these yummy sweets are chock full of cholesterol-free soy. All are satisfying, delicious, and perfect for the health-conscious eater. Finally, you can have your cake and eat it, too! Bon appétit!

the soy dessert & baking book

**good sources of protein are found in the
following commonly used soyfoods:**

. . . .

4 ounces firm tofu: 13 grams

. . . .

4 ounces soft or silken tofu: 9 grams

. . . .

8 ounces plain soy milk: 10 grams

. . . .

½ cup roasted soynuts: 39 grams

. . . .

Courtesy of The United Soybean Board

use fresh ingredients

It is important to buy good quality, fresh ingredients that contain all their healthy
nutrients and have not been exposed to salmonella contamination. Eggs, for example,
should be extra fresh when they are used in their raw state to make desserts (such as
mousses and creams) that require no cooking. In order to avoid all risk of contamination, I suggest that you use liquid eggs as a replacement for fresh eggs in these kinds
of recipes as I have done, for example, in the Holiday Eggnog (page 200).

a word about the nutritional analysis

You'll notice that in several recipes in *The Soy Dessert and Baking Book*, there are asterisks following some of the nutritional values. These asterisks indicate that those particular data totals were calculated with some values not available. This may result in an
underreporting of values.

a word about recipes designated as "non-dairy"

Some recipes identified as non-dairy may include butter, which I distinguish from traditional milk and dairy products such as heavy cream, sour cream, and yogurt.

introduction

the soy baker's pantry

I HAVE used more than a dozen different soy ingredients in the recipes for this book. Although their availability varies, you should have no trouble finding all of these ingredients at health food stores and the health-oriented supermarkets that have opened in many communities. Most conventional supermarkets and traditional grocery stores are likely to have, at the very least, soy milk and tofu. For each soy ingredient below, be aware that it can be substituted for its traditional counterpart in most other recipes, enabling you to make soy a regular addition to your daily diet.

soy flour   Protein-rich soy flour is made from ground soybeans. According to the Canadian Soyfoods Directory (1997), it contains two to three times more protein than wheat flour and is an excellent source of iron, vitamin B, calcium, and fiber.

Soy flour is available in both a full-fat and defatted form. Full-fat soy flour contains 21 grams of fat per 100 grams of flour; defatted soy flour contains 1 gram of fat per 100 grams of flour. Defatted soy flour contains more protein than the full-fat variety. I have used defatted soy flour for all the recipes in this book with excellent results. One tablespoon of cholesterol-free soy flour mixed with one tablespoon of water can replace one egg in baking recipes. I have reduced the egg and/or egg yolk content wherever possible without altering the taste or texture of the finished product. To thicken things like sauces and puddings, soy flour need not be mixed with other flours, but can be used on its own.

> **HINT:** Because soy flour is gluten-free and is a fine, dense powder, it cannot be used on its own in baking. For delicious, light-textured breads and pastries, replace no more than 20 to 30 percent of the flour in the recipe with soy flour.

Soy flour is readily available in many supermarkets, bulk, and health food stores. To maintain freshness, buy in modest quantities—only as much as you'd expect to use in a month—and store in an airtight container.

tofu "Meat without bones" is how the ancient Chinese referred to tofu. Tofu is soybean curd made from coagulated soy milk that forms curds that are then pressed into blocks. The resulting tofu typically comes in several different textures: soft or silken, medium, firm, and extra firm. Protein and fat content vary according to the texture of the tofu. The extra firm (most dense) variety has the highest protein, fat, and caloric content while the soft variety, because of its high water content, has the lowest. All types of tofu can be used in cooking and baking to replace a portion of the eggs and fat.

Tofu can be incorporated into virtually any dessert and baked good. It blends invisibly with other ingredients and absorbs their flavors. To achieve a smooth consistency, soft and medium tofu should be mashed or puréed before mixing with other ingredients. An electric hand mixer also works well. The resulting creamy smooth tofu makes it an ideal partial substitute for rich whipped cream, sour cream, frostings, and toppings, as I've done in the Best Whipped Topping (page 170). Tofu is available water-packed in the produce or dairy section of most supermarkets. I look for an expiration date a week beyond the purchase date. It also comes vacuum-packed with an extended shelf life. Both types must be refrigerated after opening and will stay fresh for about one week.

soynuts Similar in flavor to peanuts, crunchy soynuts or roasted soybeans are an excellent source of protein, isoflavones, and fiber. Available in plain, sweet, or salty flavors, soynuts constitute a healthy snack either on their own or mixed into cereal, as I've used them in the Granola Snack (page 102). They are also a tasty addition to breads, muffins, squares, creams, confections, and dessert toppings. Use soynuts as you would any other nut, only more sparingly because they have a strong flavor that can easily overpower a dish. When a recipe calls for crushed soynuts, crush them with a rolling pin or finely chop them in a food processor.

soy milk Soy milk is one of the most popular, versatile, and readily available soy products and certainly the easiest to use in your cooking. Soy milk can be substituted for cow's milk in any recipe without altering the flavor or texture of the dish. Soy milk contains fourteen essential nutrients, is lactose- and cholesterol-free, low in saturated fats, and is available in whole, low-fat, and nonfat varieties. The nutritional analysis for the recipes in this book reflect my use of low-fat soy milk.

Soy milk comes in a variety of flavors. For the recipes in this book, I have mostly used plain or vanilla flavored soy milk. Like cow's milk, soy milk must be refrigerated and will spoil if kept beyond the expiration date. Unless you drink or use soy milk daily in your cooking and baking, it is best to keep a minimal amount on hand. Consider buying small, individual-size cartons rather than the larger cartons.

HINT: When a recipe calls for vanilla soy milk, you can add one or two teaspoons of vanilla extract to plain soy milk; for chocolate flavored soy milk, just add cocoa.

One of the advantages of using soy milk in your cooking is that it does not curdle when mixed with lemon juice (or other acidic ingredients), as does cow's milk. This comes in handy when making fruit-based sauces and puddings.

Soy milk is easily found at any major supermarket or grocery store.

soy milk powder   Like powdered cow's milk, soy milk powder can be dissolved in water to make a nourishing beverage. It is convenient for people who do not consume soy milk on a daily basis because the powdered form can be stored in an airtight container in the refrigerator for several months without spoiling. Reconstituted soy milk powder can be used instead of regular soy milk in all of the recipes in this book that call for soy milk, and can also be used as a substitute in any recipe that calls for cow's milk.

To reduce the fat content of confections, I suggest replacing dairy cream with a combination of soy milk and soy milk powder. The melt-in-your-mouth Chocolate Caramel Truffles (page 184) get their creamy texture from this winning combination.

Soy milk powder can be obtained at most bulk and health food stores as well as at certain supermarkets.

soy protein isolate   The protein extracted from defatted soy flakes is a powdery substance called soy protein isolate. It is the purest form of soybean protein, and according to The United Soybean Board, contains approximately 90 percent protein. Rich in essential amino acids, soy protein isolate is a healthy food ingredient necessary for the growth and maintenance of the human body.

For an extra dose of soy, add soy protein isolate to beverages such as protein berry shake (page 194), cereals, and baking.

Soy protein isolate can be found in the bulk section of your health food store.

soy cream cheese   Soy cream cheese is a delicious and versatile soy food similar in taste and texture to dairy cream cheese. It can be eaten on its own, as a spread, or mixed into cake batters, fillings, creams, frostings, and toppings. Cholesterol-free and low in saturated fats, soy cream cheese blends wonderfully with other ingredients. Cheesecake with Swirled Lemon Curd (page 48) is a perfect example of how soy cream cheese can be used to make a light yet rich-tasting cake, in this case one that contains a mere 3.7 grams of saturated fat and 250 calories per serving.

Soy cream cheese is available in some supermarkets and most health food stores.

soy yogurt   A tasty alternative to dairy yogurt, soy yogurt is made by adding live bacteria cultures to soy milk and is recommended for people who are lactose intolerant. Soy or dairy yogurt can be used interchangeably in the recipes in this book. It's available in plain, vanilla, and fruit flavors, in both single serving and larger sizes, and in whole or low-fat varieties. Like its dairy counterpart, soy yogurt requires refrigeration and once opened will stay fresh for several days.

Soy yogurt is not yet as widely available as soy milk, but it is increasingly found in well-stocked health food stores and health-oriented supermarkets.

soy sour cream   Use this cholesterol-free sour cream as you would dairy sour cream in dips, sauces, pie fillings, puddings, pastries, and toppings. Its smooth, creamy texture and slightly tart flavor allow it to be used interchangeably with regular sour cream.

Soy sour cream is available in health food stores and in some supermarkets.

textured soy protein (tsp)   Usually used in meat analogs such as soy sausage and hamburgers, TSP (or TVP for Textured Vegetable Protein) is a soy product made from soy flour after the soybean oil has been extracted, then cooked under pressure, extruded, and dried. TSP is cholesterol-free, rich in protein, vitamin B_{12}, and iron. It is low in sodium and fat and is an excellent source of fiber. TSP resembles ground meat when reconstituted and can also be used as a thickening agent in certain puddings and pies, as I have done in the Butter Tart recipe (page 75).

TSP is available in dehydrated form in bulk and health food stores. It keeps well in an airtight container and does not require refrigeration.

soy flakes   Soy flakes are thinly sliced soybeans resembling sliced almonds, only finer and smaller. I've used soy flakes in many of the recipes in this book as a partial or complete substitution for nuts. To bring out their nutty flavor, I generally toast them briefly (a few minutes at the most) in a toaster oven before adding them to a recipe. High in protein, isoflavones, and fiber, soy flakes are a nutritious and flavorful addition to a wide variety of baked goods, desserts, and confections.

Soy flakes are available in bulk and health food stores. They can be stored in the refrigerator in an airtight container for several months.

soynut butter   Made from ground soynuts, soynut butter is a delicious alternative to peanut butter, especially for people who are allergic to peanuts, and its fat content is slightly lower. Soynut butter has a strong, full-bodied, nutty flavor. When substituting it for peanut butter in a recipe, I reduce the quantity called for by about one half (otherwise the strong taste will overpower the recipe). I like to use soynut butter in icings, cookies, and confections.

Soynut butter is available at health food stores and in many supermarkets.

soybean oil   This lightly flavored, cholesterol-free oil, extracted from whole soybeans, is an excellent cooking and baking oil. I've used it in most of the quick bread and muffin recipes found in this book. Soybean oil contains linoleic and linoleic fatty acids, two polyunsaturated fatty acids essential to good health, and is very low in saturated fats.

Soybean oil is available at health food stores and in most supermarkets.

soy margarine   Made from soybean oil, soy margarine is convenient to use in baking if one cannot tolerate butter. Like soybean oil, soy margarine is cholesterol-free and contains an extremely small amount of saturated fat. Recent studies suggest that non-hydrogenated soy margarine is healthier than the hydrogenated form.

Soy margarine is available in all supermarkets.

cookies

double chocolate chip cookies

A HEALTHIER version of a classic chocolate chip cookie variety, these lightly sweetened cake-like cookies take about as long to make as a ready-mix. And I bet they will disappear just as quickly!

3 oz.	semi-sweet chocolate, coarsely chopped	85 g
2 tbsp.	vanilla soy milk	30 mL
2 tbsp.	butter, cut up	30 mL
1/4 cup	packed brown sugar	60 mL
2	eggs, beaten	2
1/2 cup	unbleached flour	125 mL
1/4 cup	soy flour	60 mL
1/4 tsp.	baking powder	1 mL
2 tbsp.	toasted soy flakes	30 mL
1/2 cup	milk chocolate chips	125 mL

- In a medium microwavable bowl, combine semisweet chocolate with soy milk. Microwave on high for 30 seconds. Stir and microwave another 30 seconds, or until chocolate is almost completely melted. Gradually stir in remaining ingredients in the order given.
- Drop cookie dough by small spoonfuls onto an ungreased nonstick or parchment-lined cookie sheet.
- Bake 10 to 12 minutes, or until cookies are puffed and done. Transfer to wire rack to cool.

makes 24–28 cookies
preparation time: 10 minutes
baking time: 10–12 minutes

PER COOKIE: 67 calories, 2 g protein, 8 g carbohydrate, 3 g total fat (1 g sat fat, 1 g mono fat, < .5 g poly fat), 16 mg cholesterol, < .5 dietary fiber, 14 RE vitamin A, 2 mcg folate, 5 mg calcium, < .5 mg iron, 23 mg potassium, 13 mg sodium

the **soy** dessert & baking book

double nut-butter cookies

A COMBINATION of half peanut butter and half soynut butter gives these cookies lots of flavor and less fat than traditional peanut butter cookies.

½ cup	butter or margarine, softened	125 mL
¼ cup	soynut butter	60 mL
¼ cup	peanut butter	60 mL
⅓ cup	firmly packed brown sugar	75 mL
⅓ cup	granulated sugar	75 mL
1	egg, beaten	1
1 tsp.	vanilla extract	5 mL
1¼ cups	unbleached flour	310 mL
¼ cup	soy flour	60 mL
½ tsp.	baking soda	2 mL
¼ tsp.	salt	1 mL

- Preheat oven to 350° F (180° C).
- In a large bowl, cream together butter, soynut butter, and peanut butter. Mix in sugars, egg, and vanilla. Gradually stir in flours, baking soda, and salt.
- Shape dough into balls (about 1 tablespoonful/15 mL), place them onto an ungreased or parchment-lined cookie sheet, and flatten them with a fork. Bake for 8 to 10 minutes.

makes about 3 dozen
preparation time: 30 minutes
baking time: 8–10 minutes
freezes well

PER COOKIE: 93 calories, 2 g protein, 8 g carbohydrate, 4 g total fat (2 g sat fat, 1 g mono fat, < .5 g poly fat), 12 mg cholesterol, < .5 dietary fiber*, 27 RE vitamin A*, 2 mcg folate*, < .5 mg vitamin C*, 4 mg calcium*, < .5 mg iron*, 20 mg potassium, 53 mg sodium

cream cheese snickerdoodles
non-dairy

THIS IS an adaptation of a recipe by Nova Scotia's favorite food editor, Marie Nightingale. These were her favorite Christmas cookies while she was growing up. My grandson Tyler likes them, too. I've scratched one egg yolk and replaced half the butter with cholesterol-free soy cream cheese.

½ cup	butter or margarine, softened	125 mL
4 oz.	soy cream cheese	125 g
1½ cups	granulated sugar	375 mL
1	egg	1
1	egg white	1
1 tsp.	vanilla extract	5 mL
2 cups	unbleached flour	500 mL
¼ cup	soy flour	60 mL
2 tsp.	cream of tartar	10 mL
1 tsp.	baking soda	5 mL
	pinch of salt	

coating

2 tbsp.	granulated sugar	30 mL
2 tsp.	ground cinnamon	10 mL

- In a large bowl, cream together butter, cream cheese, and sugar. Beat in egg, egg white, and vanilla. Gradually add dry ingredients and stir just until combined. Cover with plastic wrap and chill at least 30 minutes or overnight.
- In a small bowl, combine sugar and cinnamon. Set aside.
- Preheat oven to 400° F (200° C).
- Shape dough into 1-inch (2.5 cm) balls. Roll balls in sugar cinnamon mixture. Place on ungreased cookie sheets 2 inches (5 cm) apart.
- Bake 8 to 10 minutes or until puffed and crinkled on top. Centers will remain soft. Store in an airtight container for up to 2 weeks.

makes 5–6 dozen cookies
preparation time: 40 minutes
baking time: 8–10 minutes
freezes well

PER COOKIE: 47 calories, 1 g protein, 7 g carbohydrate, 2 g total fat (1 g sat fat, < .5 g mono fat, < .5 g poly fat), 6 mg cholesterol, < .5 g dietary fiber, 14 RE vitamin A, < .5 mcg folate, 1 mg calcium, < .5 mg iron, 16 mg potassium, 21 mg sodium

non-dairy, 1-bowl recipe

THIS VARIATION on the already wholesome oatmeal-raisin cookie makes a classic even more satisfying.

½ cup	butter or margarine, softened	125 mL
¼ cup	soft tofu	60 mL
½ cup	granulated sugar	125 mL
½ cup	packed brown sugar	125 mL
1	egg	1
2 tbsp.	water	30 mL
2 tsp.	vanilla	10 mL
¾ cup	unbleached flour	175 mL
¼ cup	soy flour	60 mL
1 tsp.	baking soda	5 mL
1 tsp.	cinnamon	5 mL
3 cups	rolled oats	750 mL
½ cup	raisins	125 mL
2 tbsp.	crushed roasted soynuts	30 mL

- Preheat oven to 350° F (180° C).
- In a large bowl, using an electric mixer or hand blender, blend together butter, tofu, sugars, egg, water, and vanilla until light and fluffy.
- Gradually beat in flours, baking soda, and cinnamon until well blended. Stir in oats, raisins, and soynuts.
- Drop dough by small spoonfuls onto an ungreased or parchment-lined nonstick cookie sheet. Press flat for crisp cookies or leave mounded for chewy ones. Bake 12 to 15 minutes, or until golden brown.

makes 50–55 cookies
preparation time: 20 minutes
baking time: 12–15 minutes
freezes well

PER COOKIE: 62 calories, 2 g protein, 9 g carbohydrate, 2 g total fat (1 g sat fat, 1 g mono fat, < .5 g poly fat), 8 mg cholesterol, 1 g dietary fiber, 17 RE vitamin A, 6 mcg folate, < .5 mg vitamin C, 5 mg calcium, < .5 mg iron, 22 mg potassium, 22 mg sodium

cranberry oatmeal cookies
non-dairy, 1-bowl recipe

OVER THE last few years vitamin C-rich dried cranberries have become more widely available year round. (Look for them at supermarkets or bulk food stores.) These soft wholesome cookies are sure to please young and old alike.

½ cup	butter or margarine, softened	125 mL
¼ cup	granulated sugar	60 mL
½ cup	liquid honey	125 mL
1	egg	1
1 tsp.	vanilla extract	5 mL
1 cup	rolled oats	250 mL
¼ cup	toasted soy flakes	60 mL
1 cup	unbleached flour	250 mL
¼ cup	soy flour	60 mL
1 tsp.	baking soda	5 mL
1 tsp.	ground cinnamon	5 mL
¼ tsp.	salt	1 mL
1 tbsp.	grated orange peel, optional	15 mL
½ cup	dried cranberries	125 mL

- Preheat oven to 350° F (180° C). Grease or line cookie sheets with parchment.
- In a large bowl, using an electric hand blender, blend together butter, sugar, honey, egg, and vanilla until smooth.
- Gradually stir in remaining ingredients. Drop by small spoonfuls onto cookie sheets. Bake 10 to 12 minutes, or until cookies are puffed and just starting to turn golden (over-baking makes cookies dry). Cool pan on wire rack for a few minutes, then remove cookies to cool directly on rack.

makes 35–40 cookies
preparation time: 15 minutes
baking time: 10–12 minutes

PER COOKIE: 60 calories, 2 g protein, 7 g carbohydrate, 3 g total fat (1 g sat fat, 1 g mono fat, < .5 g poly fat), 11 mg cholesterol, 1 g dietary fiber, 24 RE vitamin A, 1 mcg folate, 1 mg vitamin C, 3 mg calcium, < .5 mg iron, 10 mg potassium, 48 mg sodium

dried fruit and oat crunchies

ENJOY THESE healthy fiber-rich cookies with a cup of your favorite tea or coffee.

6 tbsp.	butter or margarine, softened	90 mL
½ cup	confectioner's sugar	125 mL
¼ cup	soy milk	60 mL
1 cup	unbleached flour	250 mL
2 tbsp.	soy flour	30 mL
¼ cup	cornstarch	60 mL
¼ cup	oats	60 mL
2 tbsp.	toasted soynuts	30 mL
⅓ cup	chopped mixed dried fruit (apricots, cranberries, apples, pears, prunes, etc.)	75 mL
	granulated sugar, for sprinkling (optional)	

- In a large bowl, cream together butter and confectioner's sugar. Stir in soy milk. Work in flours, cornstarch, oats, soynuts, and dried fruit with hands to form a soft smooth dough. Shape into two 6-inch (15 cm) logs. Wrap each log in foil and refrigerate at least 30 minutes or overnight.
- Preheat oven to 325° F (165° C). Slice each log into 15 rounds, re-shaping as necessary if dough is crumbly. Place on ungreased or parchment-lined cookie sheet. Sprinkle with a little sugar, if desired.
- Bake 15 to 20 minutes or until edge of cookies is lightly browned. Remove from cookie sheet with a spatula and cool on wire rack.

makes 28–32 cookies
preparation time: 20 minutes
baking time: 15–20 minutes
freezes well

PER COOKIE: 53 calories, 1 g protein, 8 g carbohydrate, 2 g total fat (1 g sat fat, 1 g mono fat, < .5 g poly fat), 6 mg cholesterol, < .5 g dietary fiber, 27 RE vitamin A, < .5 mcg folate, < .5 mg vitamin C, 2 mg calcium, < .5 mg iron, 25 mg potassium, 1 mg sodium

ginger cookies
non-dairy

JUST AS tofu and ginger go hand-in-hand in Asian stir-fries, so do soy flour and ginger in cookies. If you really love the taste of ginger, feel free to add more.

2 cups	unbleached flour	500 mL
¼ cup	soy flour	60 mL
1 tsp.	baking soda	5 mL
½ tsp.	salt	2 mL
½ tsp.	ground ginger	2 mL
½ tsp.	ground cinnamon	2 mL
6 tbsp.	butter or margarine, softened	90 mL
⅓ cup	packed brown sugar	75 mL
1	egg	1
½ cup	corn syrup	125 mL
2 tbsp.	orange juice	30 mL
2 tbsp.	finely chopped crystallized ginger	30 mL
2 tbsp.	crushed honey-roasted soynuts	30 mL
1–2 tbsp.	soy milk	15–30 mL
	granulated sugar, as a topping (optional)	

- Preheat oven to 350° F (180° C). Line cookie sheets with parchment paper or grease lightly.
- In a medium bowl, combine flours, baking soda, salt, ground ginger, and cinnamon.
- In a large bowl, cream together butter and brown sugar until smooth. Beat in egg, corn syrup, orange juice, and crystallized ginger. Gradually work in flour mixture and soynuts until dough sticks together. If dough is too dry, add a little soy milk.
- Shape dough into 1-inch (2.5 cm) balls and place them on cookie sheets 2 inches (5 cm) apart. Flatten each ball slightly with the bottom of a glass dipped in sugar.
- Bake 10 to 12 minutes or until puffed and golden. Cool on wire rack. Store in an airtight container for up to 2 weeks.

makes 40–50 cookies
preparation time: 30 minutes
baking time: 10–12 minutes
freezes well

PER COOKIE: 50 calories, 1 g protein, 8 g carbohydrate, 2 g total fat (1 g sat fat, < .5 g mono fat, < .5 g poly fat), 7 mg cholesterol, < .5 g dietary fiber, 45 RE vitamin A, 1 mcg folate, < .5 mg vitamin C, 4 mg calcium, < .5 mg iron, 12 mg potassium, 50 mg sodium

the soy dessert & baking book

chinese almond cookies

I ALWAYS enjoy almond cookies with oolong tea when we go out for Chinese food. I have replaced the lard in traditional almond cookies with a combination of butter and soy cream cheese.

5 tbsp.	butter or margarine, softened	75 mL
5 tbsp.	soy cream cheese	75 mL
1/2 cup	granulated sugar	125 mL
1/4 cup	packed brown sugar	60 mL
1	egg	1
1 tbsp.	almond extract	15 mL
2 1/4 cups	unbleached flour	560 mL
1/4 cup	soy flour	60 mL
1/4 tsp.	baking soda	1 mL
1/4 tsp.	salt	1 mL
2 tbsp.	soy milk	30 mL
40	whole, blanched almonds	40
	granulated sugar, for sprinkling (optional)	

- In a large bowl, cream together butter, cream cheese, and sugars. Add egg and almond extract. Gradually sift flours, baking soda, and salt into creamed mixture and work in with electric mixer or by hand until dough holds together. Shape dough into a 4-inch (10 cm) log and cut it into 2 equal portions.
- Place each portion in the middle of separate sheets of wax paper or plastic wrap. Roll each log into a 9-inch (23 cm) cylinder and wrap tightly. Chill at least 4 hours or overnight (dough can be frozen for later use).
- Preheat oven to 275° F (135° C). Cut each roll into 20 slices. Place slices on ungreased cookie sheets. Brush with soy milk, press an almond into center of each cookie, and sprinkle with a little sugar, if desired.
- Bake 20 to 25 minutes. Increase oven temperature to 325° F (165° C) and continue to bake another 10 minutes, or until cookies are lightly browned. Transfer cookies to wire rack and cool completely before storing in an airtight container.

makes about 40 cookies
preparation time: 20 minutes
chilling time: 4 hours to overnight
baking time: 30–35 minutes

PER COOKIE: 69 calories, 2 g protein, 9 g carbohydrate, 3 g total fat (1 g sat fat, 1 g mono fat, 1 g poly fat), 9 mg cholesterol, < .5 g dietary fiber, 16 RE vitamin A, 1 mcg folate, 5 mg calcium, 1 mg iron, 17 mg potassium, 31 mg sodium

lemon cookies

COOKIES GENERALLY require a lot of butter (or other shortening) in order for them to have the right texture and flavor. Not so with these buttery lemon flavored cookies where I've substituted ½ cup of butter with a combination of tofu, extra lemon juice, and roasted soynuts. They are addictively good and disappear quickly every time I make them.

½ cup	butter, softened	125 mL
¼ cup	soft margarine	60 mL
½ cup	granulated sugar	125 mL
½ cup	confectioner's sugar	125 mL
2 tbsp.	grated lemon peel	30 mL
3 tbsp.	lemon juice	45 mL
1½ cups	unbleached flour	375 mL
½ cup	soy flour	125 mL
½ tsp.	baking powder	2 mL
	pinch of salt	
¼ cup	roasted soynuts, chopped or crushed	60 mL
	sugar, for sprinkling (optional)	

- In a large bowl, beat butter, margarine, and sugars until creamy. Fold in lemon peel and juice. Add flours, baking powder, salt, and soynuts. Knead until dough sticks together, forming a ball. Cut dough in half and shape into two 6-inch (15 cm) long logs. Wrap each log tightly in foil and refrigerate until ready to use, at least 4 hours or overnight.
- Preheat oven to 350° F (180° C). Keeping 1 log refrigerated, cut the other log into ¼-inch (.5 cm) thick slices. Place slices on ungreased or parchment-lined cookie sheet about 1 inch (2.5 cm) apart. Sprinkle with sugar, if desired.
- Bake 10 to 12 minutes, or until lightly browned around the edges. Let cool for 2 minutes, then, with spatula, transfer cookies to wire rack. Repeat with remaining dough. Cool completely before storing in airtight container. Cookies will keep for up to 2 weeks.

makes 4–5 dozen cookies
preparation time: 25 minutes
chilling time: 4 hours to overnight
baking time: 10–12 minutes per batch

PER COOKIE: 43 calories, 1 g protein, 5 g carbohydrate, 2 g total fat (1 g sat fat, < .5 g mono fat, < .5 g poly fat), 4 mg cholesterol, < .5 g dietary fiber, 14 RE vitamin A, < .5 mcg folate, 1 mg vitamin C, 2 mg calcium, < .5 mg iron, 2 mg potassium, 14 mg sodium

coconut macaroons

FRIENDS AND family tell me these moist, soft, and chewy macaroons are the best they have ever tasted. The secret is in letting the dough rest long enough for the coconut and soy flakes to absorb the creamy soy milk/flour mixture before putting it in a hot oven.

¼ cup	soy flour	60 mL
¼ cup	vanilla soy milk	60 mL
1 cup	granulated sugar	250 mL
2	egg whites	2
2¼ cups	unsweetened shredded coconut	560 mL
2 tbsp.	soy flakes	30 mL

- In a medium bowl, using an electric hand blender, blend together flour, soy milk, sugar, and egg whites. Fold in coconut and soy flakes. Cover and let rest for 30 minutes for coconut to absorb liquid.
- Preheat oven to 375° F (190° C). Line cookie sheets with parchment paper.
- Drop dough by small spoonfuls onto cookie sheet, about 2 inches (5 cm) apart.
- Bake 12 to 15 minutes, or until puffed and lightly browned around the edges. Cool completely, then gently peel off parchment paper. Store in an airtight container for up to 2 weeks.

makes about 35 cookies
preparation time: 10 minutes
resting time: 30 minutes
baking time: 12–15 minutes

PER MACAROON: 60 calories, 1 g protein, 9 g carbohydrate, 2 g total fat (2 g sat fat, < .5 g mono fat, < .5 g poly fat), < .5 g dietary fiber, < .5 RE vitamin A, 1 mcg folate, < .5 mg vitamin C, 1 mg calcium, < .5 mg iron, 26 mg potassium, 19 mg sodium

lemon coconut biscotti

non-dairy

MY DAUGHTER couldn't wait to taste these light crunchy biscotti when she smelled them baking in the oven the first time I made them with soy ingredients. I love to dunk them in soy milk or coffee.

¼ cup	butter or margarine, softened	60 mL
½ cup	granulated sugar	125 mL
¼ cup	soft or medium tofu	60 mL
2	eggs	2
1½ cups	unbleached flour	375 mL
½ cup	soy flour	125 mL
2 tsp.	baking powder	10 mL
¼ tsp.	salt	1 mL
1 tbsp.	grated lemon peel	15 mL
2 tbsp.	toasted soy flakes	30 mL
¼ cup	chopped dried citrus peel	60 mL
¼ cup	unsweetened shredded coconut	60 mL

- Preheat oven to 350° F (180° C).
- In a large bowl, cream together butter and sugar. Using an electric mixer or hand blender, add tofu and eggs, beating until smooth. Gradually add flours, baking powder, and salt. Work in lemon peel, soy flakes, dried citrus peel, and coconut. Form dough into a ball. Place ball on lightly floured work surface and cut in half. Shape each half into a 10-inch (25 cm) log, slightly rounded on top. Place logs 3 inches (7.5 cm) apart on an ungreased nonstick baking sheet.
- Bake in center of oven for 30 minutes, or until light golden and not quite firm to the touch. Cool on baking sheet for 10 minutes.
- Place logs on a cutting board and, with a sharp serrated knife, cut each log diagonally into 16 to 18 slices. Place flat on baking sheet.

- Bake 10 minutes; turn over biscotti and bake another 10 minutes, or until lightly browned around the edges and firm. Remove from baking sheet and cool on wire racks.
- Store in an airtight container for up to 2 weeks.

makes 32–36 biscotti
preparation time: 20 minutes
baking time: about 50 minutes
freezes well

PER BISCOTTI: 66 calories, 2 g protein, 8 g carbohydrate, 3 g total fat (2 g sat fat, 1 g mono fat, < .5 g poly fat), 14 mg cholesterol, 1 g dietary fiber, 18 RE vitamin A, 2 mcg folate, 1 mg vitamin C, 6 mg calcium, 1 mg iron, 19 mg potassium, 37 mg sodium

nutty meringues

THESE MELT-IN-YOUR-MOUTH delicacies can be whipped up any time you have a couple of leftover egg whites.

2	egg whites, at room temperature	2
¹⁄₄ tsp.	vanilla extract	1 mL
	pinch of cream of tartar	
1¹⁄₂ cups	confectioner's sugar	375 mL
2 tbsp.	crushed roasted soynuts	30 mL
¹⁄₂ cup	coarsely chopped macadamia and/or Brazil nuts	125 mL

- Preheat oven to 325° F (165° C). Line cookie sheets with parchment paper.
- In a large bowl, beat egg whites with vanilla and cream of tartar until soft peaks form. Gradually beat in confectioner's sugar until smooth. Fold in soy and macadamia nuts. Drop mixture by rounded teaspoonfuls 2 inches (5 cm) apart on parchment-lined cookie sheets.
- Bake meringues about 15 minutes, or until puffed and golden. Peel off parchment paper and cool on wire rack.

makes 28–32 meringues
preparation time: 10 minutes
baking time: 15 minutes

PER MERINGUE: 42 calories, 1 g protein, 6 g carbohydrate, 2 g total fat (< .5 g sat fat, 1 g mono fat, < .5 g poly fat), < .5 g dietary fiber, < .5 mcg folate, < .5 mg vitamin C, 3 mg calcium, < .5 mg iron, 11 mg potassium, 11 mg sodium

COCONUT, CHOCOLATE chips, and soynuts enveloped in a sweet meringue. Yummy!

2	egg whites, at room temperature	2
	pinch of cream of tartar	
1 1/2 cups	confectioner's sugar	750 mL
1/2 cup	unsweetened shredded coconut	125 mL
2 tbsp.	crushed roasted soynuts	30 mL
2 tbsp.	chocolate chips	30 mL

- Preheat oven to 325° F (165° C). Line cookie sheets with parchment paper.
- In a large bowl, beat egg whites with cream of tartar until soft peaks form. Gradually beat in confectioner's sugar until stiff. Fold in coconut, soynuts, and chocolate chips. Drop mixture by rounded teaspoonfuls, 2 inches (5 cm) apart, on lined cookie sheets.
- Bake meringues about 15 minutes, or until puffed and golden. Peel meringues off parchment paper and cool on wire rack.

makes 28–32 meringues
preparation time: 10 minutes
baking time: 15 minutes

PER MERINGUE: 38 calories, 1 g protein, 7 g carbohydrate, 1 g total fat (1 g sat fat, < .5 g mono fat, < .5 g poly fat), < .5 g dietary fiber, 1 RE vitamin A, < .5 mcg folate, < .5 mg vitamin C, 2 mg calcium, < .5 mg iron, 8 mg potassium, 15 mg sodium

lace brandy cups

non-dairy

MORE LIKE a confection than cookies, these attractive lace cookie cups are very easy to bake but a little difficult to shape. Once you've mastered the technique, though, they're a snap to make. Their crunchy texture and rich buttery flavor make them a good foil for a variety of fillings.

5 tbsp.	unbleached flour	75 mL
1 tbsp.	soy flour	15 mL
1 tbsp.	soy flakes	15 mL
1/4 tsp.	ground ginger	1 mL
1/4 cup	butter or margarine	60 mL
1/4 cup	corn syrup	60 mL
2 tbsp. + 2 tsp.	packed brown sugar	40 mL
2 tsp.	brandy	10 mL

- Have 6 to 8 inverted glasses (2 to 2½ inches/5–6 cm. in diameter) ready on work surface to shape cookies.
- Preheat oven to 350° F (180° C). Cover cookie sheet with parchment paper.
- In a small bowl, combine flours, soy flakes, and ginger.
- In a small saucepan, bring butter, corn syrup, and brown sugar to a boil while stirring. Remove from heat. Stir in brandy, then stir in flour mixture.
- Drop heaping teaspoonfuls of batter onto baking sheet 4 inches (10 cm) apart. Bake in 2 batches to allow time to shape cookies.
- Bake 4 minutes, or until cookies have spread into 4- to 5-inch (10–12 cm) rounds and are bubbly and golden brown. Let cool about 2 minutes until they hold together when handled. Quickly place cookies over inverted glasses and shape into cups by pinching 3 or 4 "pleats" near the base. Let cookies harden before transferring them to wire racks to cool.
- Shortly before serving, fill cups with berries or cut-up fruit and top with your favorite cream such as Best Whipped Topping, page 170 or Grand Marnier Cream Filling, page 44.

makes 12–15 cookie cups
preparation time: batter, 5 minutes
shaping, 15 minutes
baking time: about 4 minutes
storing: will keep in an airtight container for up to 2 weeks

VARIATIONS: Instead of shaping cookies into cups, make them smaller and just bake them as regular cookies or pour all the batter into a thin layer on a parchment-lined cookie sheet, bake, let cool, and break into pieces.

PER CUP: 67 calories, 1 g protein, 9 g carbohydrate, 3 g total fat (2 g sat fat, 1 g mono fat, < .5 g poly fat), 8 mg cholesterol, < .5 g dietary fiber, 29 RE vitamin A, < .5 mcg folate, 3 mg calcium, < .5 mg iron, 10 mg potassium, 2 mg sodium

wonton cinnamon crisps

NOT ONLY will kids love to eat these crisps, they will also want to make them. This is a perfect recipe for first-time bakers as it is easy and fun to prepare. The soy milk replaces the butter.

15	wonton wrappers	15
1 tbsp.	soy milk	15 mL
1–2 tbsp.	granulated sugar	15–30 mL
1–2 tsp.	cinnamon	5–10 mL

- Preheat oven to 400° F (200° C). Grease a large baking sheet.
- Cut each wonton diagonally into 2 triangles. Place on baking sheet ½ inch (1½ cm) apart. Brush triangles with soy milk. Combine sugar and cinnamon and sprinkle over wontons.
- Bake 5 to 7 minutes, or until lightly browned. Cool on wire rack.

makes 30 crisps
preparation time: 15 minutes
baking time: 5–7 minutes

PER CRISP: 14 calories, < .5 g protein, 3 g carbohydrate, < .5 g total fat (< .5 g sat fat, < .5 g mono fat, < .5 g poly fat), < .5 mg cholesterol, < .5 g dietary fiber, < .5 RE vitamin A, 3 mcg folate, < .5 mg vitamin C, 3 mg calcium, < .5 mg iron, 4 mg potassium, 23 mg sodium

squares & bars

chocolate brownies
non-dairy

I INCLUDED a recipe for chocolate brownies in *Tofu Mania* but those aren't dairy-free. So, I've developed a non-dairy recipe for this book. I've added soy flour and soy flakes to the batter, and reduced the butter in the icing. No matter the changes, the chocolatey taste and fudgy texture remain the same.

1½ cups	granulated sugar	375 mL
½ cup	butter or margarine	125 mL
½ cup	soft tofu	125 mL
½ cup	soy milk	125 mL
2	eggs	2
1 tsp.	vanilla extract	5 mL
¼ cup	soy flour	60 mL
¾ cup	unbleached flour	175 mL
¾ cup	unsweetened cocoa powder	175 mL
¾ tsp.	baking powder	3 mL
½ tsp.	salt	2 mL
½ cup	chopped walnuts or pecans	125 mL
2 tbsp.	toasted soy flakes	30 mL
	Chocolate Frosting, below	

chocolate frosting

1 cup	confectioner's sugar	250 mL
¼ cup	unsweetened cocoa powder	60 mL
1 tbsp.	butter, softened	15 mL
2–3 tsp.	soy milk	30–45 mL

- *To make the frosting,* cream all ingredients together in a small bowl to spreading consistency.
- Preheat oven to 350° F (180° C). Grease a 9 x 13-inch (23 x 33 cm) baking dish.
- In a medium bowl, using an electric mixer or hand blender, beat sugar, butter, and tofu until smooth. Beat in soy milk, eggs, and vanilla. Gradually mix in flours, cocoa, baking powder, and salt until smooth. Fold in walnuts and soy flakes.
- Spread batter evenly in prepared baking dish. Bake about 30 minutes, or until tooth-pick inserted in center comes out clean. Let cool in pan on wire rack.
- Spread frosting over brownies with a metal spatula while brownies are still slightly warm. Cool completely; cut into squares.

makes 24 brownies
preparation time: 15 minutes
baking time: 30 minutes
freezes well

PER BROWNIE: 165 calories, 4 g protein, 24 g carbohydrate, 7 g total fat (3 g sat fat, 2 g mono fat, 1 g poly fat), 27 mg cholesterol, 2 g dietary fiber, 48 RE vitamin A, 6 mcg folate, < .5 mg vitamin C, 12 mg calcium, 1 mg iron, 91 mg potassium, 65 mg sodium

brownie cheesecake squares
non-dairy

CHOCOLATE BROWNIES and cheesecake—two delectable cakes mixed into one. Yummy! The cheesecake layer consists primarily of soy ingredients, yet tastes exactly like regular cheesecake.

brownie layer

2 tbsp.	soybean oil	30 mL
¼ cup	granulated sugar	60 mL
¼ cup	unsweetened cocoa powder	60 mL
¼ cup	brown sugar	60 mL
¼ cup	unsweetened applesauce	60 mL
1	egg	1
1 tsp.	vanilla extract	5 mL
¼ tsp.	salt	1 mL
¼ tsp.	baking powder	1 mL
¼ cup	soy flour	60 mL
¼ cup	unbleached flour	60 mL

cheesecake layer

4 oz.	(½ container) soy cream cheese	125 g
½ cup	soft tofu	125 mL
2	eggs	2
2 tbsp.	soy flour	30 mL

- Preheat oven to 350° F (180° C). Grease an 8-inch (20 cm) square pan.
- *Brownie layer:* In a medium bowl, using an electric mixer or hand blender, blend all ingredients in the order given until smooth. Reserve ¼ cup (60 mL) and set aside. Spread remaining batter evenly in pan.
- *Cheesecake layer:* In a medium bowl, using an electric mixer or hand blender, combine all ingredients until smooth. Pour over the brownie layer, reserving a couple of teaspoons.
- Add the reserved brownie batter to the remaining cheesecake batter and mix lightly; then drop it by small spoonfuls across the cheesecake layer.
- Bake 25 minutes or until the sides are somewhat set and a toothpick inserted in the center comes out slightly moist.

makes 9 squares
preparation time: 15–20 minutes
baking time: 25 minutes

PER SQUARE: 164 calories, 6 g protein, 17 g carbohydrate, 9 g total fat (2 g sat fat, 1 g mono fat, 3 g poly fat), 62 mg cholesterol, 1 g dietary fiber, 34 RE vitamin A, 8 mcg folate, 3 mg vitamin C, 18 mg calcium, 2 mg iron, 103 mg potassium, 156 mg sodium

cherry chocolate chip cheesecake squares
non-dairy

A HINT of chocolate in this lightly sweetened filling will satisfy the cravings of chocolate lovers without making them feel guilty.

	Basic Shortbread Crust, page 60	
8 oz.	soy cream cheese	250 g
1 cup	soft tofu	250 mL
½ cup	granulated sugar	125 mL
1	egg	1
1 tbsp.	soy flour	15 mL
¼–½ cup	semi-sweet chocolate chips	60–125 mL
1½ cups	pitted sour cherries, fresh or frozen	375 mL
¼ cup	cherry juice	60 mL

- Preheat oven to 400° F (200° C).
- Make Basic Shortbread Crust and press into greased 9-inch (23 cm) square cake pan. Cover with foil and bake 15 minutes.
- Meanwhile, using an electric mixer or hand blender, blend together cream cheese, tofu, sugar, egg, and flour until smooth. Fold in chocolate chips, sour cherries, and juice. Pour over hot crust. Reduce oven temperature to 350° F (180° C). Bake, uncovered, 20 minutes, or until filling has set. Cool in pan on wire rack. Cut into squares.

makes 9–12 servings
preparation time: crust, 15 minutes
filling, 10 minutes
baking time: about 35 minutes
freezes well

PER SERVING: 214 calories, 6 g protein, 24 g carbohydrate, 11 g total fat (3 g sat fat, 1 g mono fat, 4 g poly fat), 23 mg cholesterol, 1 g dietary fiber, 59 RE vitamin A, 3 mcg folate, < .5 mg vitamin C, 12 mg calcium, 1 mg iron, 86 mg potassium, 98 mg sodium

white chocolate cherry bars

ANYONE WITH a sweet tooth will want to indulge in these incredibly good treats.

½ cup	butter or margarine, softened	125 mL
1 cup	packed brown sugar	250 mL
1	egg	1
1	egg white	1
½ cup	soy sour cream	125 mL
½ cup	soft tofu, mashed	125 mL
1 tsp.	vanilla extract	5 mL
2 cups	unbleached flour	500 mL
¼ cup	soy flour	60 mL
1½ tsp.	baking powder	7 mL
½ tsp.	baking soda	2 mL
¼ tsp.	salt	1 mL
6 oz.	white chocolate, chopped, divided	170 g
1 cup	dried Bing Cherries	250 mL
½ cup	chopped nuts	125 mL
2 tbsp.	toasted soy flakes	30 mL

- Preheat oven to 350° F (180° C). Grease a 9 x 13-inch (23 x 33 cm) baking pan.
- In a medium bowl, beat together first 7 ingredients until smooth and creamy. Gradually stir in flours, baking powder, baking soda, and salt. When smooth, fold in 4 oz. (125 g) chocolate, cherries, nuts, and soy flakes. Transfer to baking dish.
- Bake about 20 minutes or until golden. Cool on wire rack.
- In a small saucepan, melt remaining 2 oz. (57 g) chocolate over low heat, stirring constantly to prevent sticking or burning. Drizzle over cooled cake. Cut into bars.

makes 36 mini or 24 regular sized bars
preparation time: 15 minutes
baking time: about 20 minutes
freezes well

PER MINI BAR: 141 calories, 3 g protein, 20 g carbohydrate, 6 g total fat (2 g sat fat, 2 g mono fat, 1 g poly fat), 12 mg cholesterol, 1 g dietary fiber, 34 RE vitamin A, 2 mcg folate, 2 mg vitamin C, 13 mg calcium, 1 mg iron, 123 mg potassium, 62 mg sodium
PER REGULAR BAR: 212 calories, 5 g protein, 30 g carbohydrate, 9 g total fat (3 g sat fat, 2 g mono fat, 1 g poly fat), 18 mg cholesterol, 2 g dietary fiber, 51 RE vitamin A, 3 mcg folate, 3 mg vitamin C, 20 mg calcium, 1 mg iron, 184 mg potassium, 93 mg sodium

sour cherry streusel squares
non-dairy

THESE "SWEET AND TART" squares have become a new favorite at our house. With frozen pitted sour cherries available all year round, these treats can be enjoyed any time.

¾ cup	unbleached flour	175 mL
¼ cup	soy flour	60 mL
¼ cup	sugar	60 mL
½ tsp.	baking powder	2 mL
	pinch of salt	
3 tbsp.	soybean oil	45 mL
1	egg	1
½ cup	soy milk	125 mL
½ cup	soft tofu	125 mL
2 tsp.	grated lemon peel	10 mL
2 cups	pitted fresh or frozen sour cherries, drained	500 mL

crumb topping

1 cup	unbleached flour	250 mL
⅓ cup	brown sugar	75 mL
¼ cup	melted butter or margarine	60 mL
2 tbsp.	honey-roasted soynuts, chopped or crushed	30 mL

- Preheat oven to 350° F (180° C). Lightly grease an 8 or 9-inch (20 or 23 cm) square cake pan.
- In a medium bowl, combine flours, sugar, baking powder, and salt.
- In a small bowl, using an electric mixer or hand blender, beat together oil, egg, soy milk, tofu, and lemon peel until smooth. Stir into dry ingredients to make a thick batter. Transfer batter to cake pan. Spread cherries evenly over top.
- To make crumb topping, combine all topping ingredients and sprinkle over fruit.
- Bake 35 to 40 minutes until topping is golden and cherries are bubbly. Cool on wire rack, then cut into squares.

makes 12 squares
preparation time: 20 minutes
baking time: 35–40 minutes

PER SQUARE: 201 calories, 6 g protein, 26 g carbohydrate, 9 g total fat (3 g sat fat, 1 g mono fat, < .5 g poly fat), 26 mg cholesterol, 2 g dietary fiber, 77 RE vitamin A, 4 mcg folate, 3 mg vitamin C, 18 mg calcium, 2 mg iron, 100 mg potassium, 40 mg sodium

the soy dessert & baking book

cranberry apple macadamia bars

I LIKE to make these bars for friends who visit during the Christmas season. One of them said they were the best she had ever tasted. That was all the encouragement I needed to include the recipe in this book!

1 cup	unbleached flour	250 mL
¼ cup	soy flour	60 mL
1½ cups	sugar, divided	375 mL
½ cup	butter or margarine, cubed	125 mL
½ cup	finely chopped macadamia nuts	125 mL
1	egg	1
1	egg white	1
¼ cup	soft tofu	60 mL
¼ cup	soy milk	60 mL
1 tsp.	grated orange peel	5 mL
½ cup	coarsely chopped macadamia nuts	125 mL
½ cup	dried cranberries	125 mL
1	medium apple, chopped	1
	sugar, for sprinkling (optional)	

- Preheat oven to 350° F (180° C). In a medium bowl, stir together flours and ½ cup (125 mL) sugar. With a pastry blender, cut in butter or margarine until mixture resembles coarse crumbs. Stir in finely chopped nuts. Press mixture into bottom of an ungreased 9 x 13-inch (23 x 33 cm) baking dish. Bake 10 minutes.

- Meanwhile, in a small bowl, using an electric hand blender, blend together remaining 1 cup (250 mL) sugar, egg, egg white, tofu, soy milk, and orange peel. Pour evenly over hot crust. Top with coarsely chopped nuts, cranberries, and chopped apple. Sprinkle with a little sugar if apples are tart.

- Bake 30 minutes or until apples are tender. Transfer to wire rack. Cut into bars while still warm.

makes 24 bars
preparation time: 30 minutes
baking time: 30 minutes
freezes well

PER BAR: 161 calories, 2 g protein, 20 g carbohydrate, 8 g total fat (3 g sat fat, 4 g mono fat, < .5 g poly fat), 18 mg cholesterol, 2 g dietary fiber, 41 RE vitamin A, 2 mcg folate, 3 mg vitamin C, 10 mg calcium, 1 mg iron, 54 mg potassium, 7 mg sodium

rum raisin and apple custard squares
non-dairy

MY DAUGHTER Bettina tells me these are among her very favorite pastries. The nutty flavored base goes well with the creamy non-dairy custard. This can be made a day ahead.

¹⁄₄ cup	raisins	60 mL
2 tbsp.	rum	30 mL
	Basic Shortbread Crust, page 60	
3–4	medium apples, peeled, cored, halved, and sliced	3–4
4 tbsp.	granulated sugar, divided	60 mL
	ground cinnamon, to taste	
4 oz.	soy cream cheese	125 g
¹⁄₂ cup	soft tofu	125 mL
1	egg	1
3 tbsp.	frozen orange juice concentrate	45 mL
1 tsp.	flour	5 mL

- In a small bowl, soak raisins in rum.
- Make Basic Shortbread Crust and press into cake pan. Preheat oven to 400° F (200°C).
- Arrange apple slices in neat rows over crust. Sprinkle apples with raisins and rum, 2 tbsp. (30 mL) sugar, and cinnamon. Cover with foil. Bake 20 minutes.
- Meanwhile, in a medium bowl, using an electric mixer or hand blender, blend together cream cheese, tofu, egg, orange juice, 1 tsp. (5 mL) flour, and remaining 2 tbsp. (30 mL) sugar until smooth. Pour over hot apples. Reduce oven temperature to 350° F (180° C). Bake, uncovered, 20 minutes, or until custard has set. Cool in pan on wire rack.

makes 9–12 squares
preparation time: 30 minutes
baking time: 40 minutes
freezes well

PER SQUARE: 178 calories, 5 g protein, 23 g carbohydrate, 7 g total fat (3 g sat fat, 1 g mono fat, 2 g poly fat), 23 mg cholesterol, 2 g dietary fiber, 39 RE vitamin A, 18 mcg folate, 1 mg vitamin C, 10 mg calcium, 1 mg iron, 127 mg potassium, 53 mg sodium

YOU'VE JUST invited a few friends over for afternoon tea but you're wondering what you could possibly bake in the hour or so before they arrive. These delicious squares take about as long to make as a simple cake mix.

¹/₂ cup	confectioner's sugar	125 mL
¹/₂ cup	brown sugar	125 mL
²/₃ cup	butter or margarine, softened	150 mL
¹/₃ cup	soy milk	75 mL
1	egg, separated	1
1 cup	unbleached flour	250 mL
¹/₂ cup	whole wheat flour	125 mL
¹/₂ cup	soy flour	125 mL
¹/₂ tsp.	ground cinnamon	2 mL
¹/₄ tsp.	ground cloves	1 mL
1 tbsp.	water	15 mL
¹/₄ cup, each	sliced almonds and chopped honey roasted soynuts	60 mL

- Preheat oven to 350° F (180° C). Grease a 9 x 13-inch (23 x 33 cm) baking dish.
- In medium bowl, cream together sugars, butter, soy milk, and egg yolk. Mix in flours, cinnamon, and cloves. Press evenly into baking dish.
- Beat egg white and water with a fork until foamy; brush over dough (only half will be needed). Sprinkle with nuts.
- Bake about 20 minutes or until edges are lightly browned. Cut into squares and let cool on wire rack.

makes 24 squares
preparation time: 15 minutes
baking time: 20 minutes

PER SQUARE: 122 calories, 4 g protein, 13 g carbohydrate, 6 g total fat (3 g sat fat, 2 g mono fat, < .5 g poly fat), 23 mg cholesterol, 1 g dietary fiber, 52 RE vitamin A, 3 mcg folate, < .5 mg vitamin C, 14 mg calcium, 1 mg iron, 37 mg potassium, 23 mg sodium

soynut butter and oat squares

non-dairy, 1-bowl recipe

THESE TASTY squares are packed with soy: soynut butter, soybean oil, soy milk, and soy flakes. When using soynut butter as a replacement for peanut butter, keep in mind that soynut butter is stronger tasting, so a little goes a long way.

½ cup	packed brown sugar	125 mL
¼ cup	granulated sugar	60 mL
¼ cup	butter or margarine, softened	60 mL
2 tbsp.	soybean oil	30 mL
2 tbsp.	soynut butter (*or* 1 tbsp. soynut butter + 2 tbsp. peanut butter)	30 mL
1	egg	1
¼ cup	soy milk	60 mL
1 cup	unbleached flour	250 mL
⅔ cup	oats	150 mL
2 tbsp.	toasted soy flakes	30 mL
½ tsp.	baking soda	2 mL
	pinch of salt	

- Preheat oven to 350° F (180° C). Grease a 9 x 13-inch (23 x 33 cm) baking dish.
- In a large bowl, cream together sugars, butter, oil, and soynut butter. Add egg and soy milk. Stir in flour, oats, soy flakes, baking soda, and salt. Spread in baking dish. Bake about 20 minutes, or until toothpick inserted in center comes out clean. Cool completely, then frost with Soynut Butter Frosting, below.

1 cup	confectioner's sugar	250 mL
1 tbsp.	soynut butter	15 mL
2 tbsp.	soy milk	30 mL

In a small bowl, mix all ingredients until smooth. If too thick to spread, add a little soy milk; if too thin, add extra confectioner's sugar.

VARIATIONS: For a marbled effect, transfer half of the frosting to a separate small bowl. Mix in 1 tbsp. (15 mL) unsweetened cocoa and 2 tsp. (10 mL) soy milk. Frost cake with the cocoa frosting. Drop small spoonfuls of the plain soynut frosting onto the cocoa frosting. Swirl a knife through the frostings to create a marbled design.

makes 24 regular or 48 mini squares
preparation time: cake, 15 minutes
frosting, 5 minutes
baking time: about 20 minutes
freezes well

PER REGULAR SQUARE: 116 calories, 2 g protein, 18 g carbohydrate, 4 g total fat (2 g sat fat, 1 g mono fat, < .5 g poly fat), 13 mg cholesterol, 1 g dietary fiber, 21 RE vitamin A, 1 mcg folate, 6 mg calcium, < .5 mg iron, 35 mg potassium, 31 mg sodium

PER MINI SQUARE: 54 calories, 1 g protein, 9 g carbohydrate, 2 g total fat (1 g sat fat, < .5 g mono fat, < .5 g poly fat), 6 mg cholesterol, < .5 g dietary fiber, 11 RE vitamin A, 1 mcg folate, 3 mg calcium, < .5 mg iron, 12 mg potassium, 11 mg sodium

crispy rice squares
non-dairy, 1-bowl recipe

CRAVING SOMETHING sweet? These fiber-rich squares will leave you satisfied without feeling guilty.

2 tbsp.	flax seeds	30 mL
¼ cup	butter or margarine	60 mL
8 oz.	mini marshmallows	250 g
1 tsp.	vanilla extract	5 mL
5 cups	crisp rice cereal	1.25 L
⅓ cup	chopped dried apricots	75 mL
⅓ cup	chopped dried apples	75 mL
⅓ cup	dried cranberries	75 mL
¼ cup	toasted soy flakes	60 mL

- Place flax seeds in a small bowl and add enough water to cover seeds. Let soak at least 1 hour.
- Grease a 9 x 13-inch (23 x 33 cm) baking dish.
- Drain flax seeds.
- In a large saucepan, over medium heat, melt butter. Stir in marshmallows, a handful at a time, until smooth. Remove from heat. Stir in vanilla. Gradually fold in remaining ingredients, including flax seeds, until evenly combined.
- Press mixture into prepared dish. Cut into squares.

makes 48 mini or 24 regular squares
soaking time: 1 hour
preparation and cooking time: 20 minutes

PER MINI SQUARE: 49 calories, 1 g protein, 9 g carbohydrate, 1 g total fat (1 g sat fat, < .5 g mono fat, < .5 g poly fat), 3 mg cholesterol, 1 g dietary fiber, 16 RE vitamin A, 1 mcg folate, 1 mg vitamin C, 2 mg calcium, < .5 mg iron, 22 mg potassium, 22 mg sodium

PER REGULAR SQUARE: 99 calories, 2 g protein, 17 g carbohydrate, 3 g total fat (1 g sat fat, 1 g mono fat, < .5 g poly fat), 5 mg cholesterol, 2 g dietary fiber, 32 RE vitamin A, 3 mcg folate, 2 mg vitamin C, 4 mg calcium, < .5 mg iron, 44 mg potassium, 44 mg sodium

lemon squares

non-dairy

MANY RECIPES for lemon squares call for lots of butter and eggs. In these airy cake-like squares I have replaced half the butter and eggs with tofu and soy milk. I usually keep some in my freezer, ready for unexpected guests. They are delicious!

¼ cup	butter or margarine, softened	60 mL
½ cup	granulated sugar	125 mL
¼ cup	soft tofu	60 mL
1	egg	1
¼ cup	soy milk	60 mL
2 tsp.	grated lemon peel	10 mL
¼ cup	fresh lemon juice	60 mL
¾ cup	unbleached flour	175 mL
¼ cup	soy flour	60 mL
2½ tsp.	baking powder	12 mL

- Preheat oven to 350° F (180° C). Grease a 9-inch (23 cm) square baking dish.
- In a medium bowl, beat together butter and sugar. Beat in tofu, egg, soy milk, lemon peel, and juice. Stir in flours and baking powder. Spread batter evenly in baking dish.
- Bake 25 to 30 minutes, or until toothpick inserted in center comes out clean. When cool, spread Lemon Glaze (below) over top of cake. Cut into squares.

lemon glaze

⅔ cup	confectioner's sugar	150 mL
1 tsp.	grated lemon peel	5 mL
2 tsp.	lemon juice	10 mL
1 tbsp.	soy milk	15 mL

- In a small bowl, mix all ingredients with a fork until smooth.

makes 12 squares
preparation time: 25 minutes
baking time: 25 to 30 minutes

PER SQUARE: 138 calories, 3 g protein, 22 g carbohydrate, 5 g total fat (3 g sat fat, 1 g mono fat, < .5 g poly fat), 26 mg cholesterol, < .5 g dietary fiber, 44 RE vitamin A, 3 mcg folate, 3 mg vitamin C, 6 mg calcium, 1 mg iron, 33 mg potassium, 68 mg sodium

peach squares
non-dairy, 1-bowl recipe

PEACHES ARE a delicate fruit, their perfect ripeness lasting only a day or two. Use bruised or over-ripe peaches in these delicious squares.

¾ cup	granulated sugar	175 mL
¼ cup	butter or margarine, softened	60 mL
¼ cup	soft tofu	60 mL
1	egg	1
1 tbsp.	frozen orange juice concentrate	15 mL
2 cups	finely chopped ripe peaches (3 to 4 peaches)	500 mL
1 cup	unbleached flour	250 mL
¼ cup	soy flour	60 mL
¼ cup	rolled oats	60 mL
1 tsp.	baking soda	5 mL
¼ cup	slivered almonds	60 mL
	Orange Glaze, below	

- Preheat oven to 350° F (180° C). Lightly grease a 9 x 13-inch (23 x 33 cm) baking dish.
- In a large bowl, beat together sugar, butter, tofu, egg, and orange juice. Fold in peaches. Stir in remaining ingredients (except for glaze). Spread batter evenly in baking dish.
- Bake 20 to 30 minutes, or until toothpick inserted in center comes out clean. When cool, spread Orange Glaze below over top of cake.

orange glaze

1½ cups	confectioner's sugar	375 mL
1½ tbsp.	frozen orange juice concentrate	22 mL
1 tbsp.	soy milk	15 mL

- In a small bowl, mix all glaze ingredients until smooth.

makes 24 squares
preparation time: 30 minutes
baking time: 20–30 minutes

PER SQUARE: 138 calories, 3 g protein, 22 g carbohydrate, 5 g total fat (3 g sat fat, 1 g mono fat, < .5 g poly fat), 26 mg cholesterol, < .5 g dietary fiber, 44 RE vitamin A, 3 mcg folate, 3 mg vitamin C, 6 mg calcium, 1 mg iron, 33 mg potassium, 68 mg sodium

cakes & frostings

light chocolate cupcakes
non-dairy

I'M WILLING to bet there won't be any leftovers when you make these moist chocolatey cakes.

1 cup	unbleached flour	250 mL
¼ cup	soy flour	60 mL
⅓ cup	unsweetened cocoa powder	75 mL
1 tsp.	baking soda	5 mL
1 tsp.	baking powder	5 mL
	pinch of salt	
¼ cup	butter or margarine, at room temperature	60 mL
1 cup	granulated sugar	250 mL
2	eggs	2
¼ cup	strong coffee	60 mL
¾ cup	vanilla soy milk	175 mL
	chocolate frosting, below	175 mL

- Preheat oven to 350° F (180° C). Line 12 muffin cups with paper cups.
- In a medium bowl, sift together flours, cocoa, baking soda, baking powder, and salt.
- Using an electric mixer or hand blender, beat butter and sugar until light. Beat in eggs. Beat in half the flour mixture, half the coffee and half the soy milk. When smooth, beat in remaining ingredients.
- Pour batter evenly into lined muffin cups. Bake about 20 minutes, or until toothpick inserted in center comes out clean. Cool on wire rack. Spread chocolate frosting, below, over tops of cooled cupcakes.

2 tbsp.	vanilla soy milk	30 mL
2 oz.	semi-sweet chocolate, coarsely chopped	56 g
¼ cup	confectioner's sugar	60 mL

- In a small saucepan, over low heat, heat soy milk and chocolate, stirring constantly to melt the chocolate. Do not boil. Remove from heat. Stir in confectioner's sugar.

makes 12 large or 24 small cupcakes
preparation time: 20 minutes
baking time: about 20 minutes for the large cupcakes,
  15 minutes for the small cupcakes
freezes well

PER LARGE CUPCAKE: 195 calories, 4 g protein, 31 g carbohydrate, 7 g total fat (3 g sat fat, 2 g mono fat, < .5 g poly fat), 42 mg cholesterol, 1 g dietary fiber, 50 RE vitamin A, 5 mcg folate, 9 mg calcium, 1 mg iron, 76 mg potassium, 106 mg sodium

PER SMALL CUPCAKE: 98 calories, 2 g protein, 16 g carbohydrate, 3 g total fat (1 g sat fat, 1 g mono fat, < .5 g poly fat), 21 mg cholesterol, 1 g dietary fiber, 25 RE vitamin A, 2 mcg folate, 4 mg calcium, 1 mg iron, 38 mg potassium, 53 mg sodium

chocolate M&M® cupcakes
non-dairy

A TAD richer and more chocolatey than the Light Chocolate Cupcakes (page 36), these treats garnished with M&Ms® (known as Smarties® in Canada) are a kid's delight. One batch of these cupcakes is never enough when my grandson Tyler has his friends over!

¹/₂ cup	soy flour	125 mL
1¹/₂ cups	unbleached flour	375 mL
³/₄ cup	unsweetened cocoa powder	175 mL
2 tsp.	baking powder	10 mL
1 tsp.	baking soda	5 mL
¹/₄ tsp.	salt	1 mL
1 cup	granulated sugar	250 mL
¹/₂ cup	butter or margarine, softened	125 mL
¹/₄ cup	soft tofu	60 mL
1	egg	1
1	egg white	1
1 cup	soy milk	250 mL
1 tsp.	vanilla	5 mL

surprise frosting

¹/₃ cup	soy cream cheese	75 mL
¹/₃ cup	soft tofu	75 mL
3 tbsp.	granulated sugar	45 mL
1	egg	1
72	M&Ms® (Smarties® in Canada) or similar candy-coated chocolate drops	72

- Preheat oven to 350° F (180° C). Line 24 medium muffin cups with paper cups.
- In a medium bowl, sift together flours, cocoa, baking powder, baking soda, and salt.
- In a large bowl, using an electric mixer or hand blender, beat sugar, butter, and tofu until creamy. Beat in egg and egg white. Alternately, beat flour mixture and soy milk into butter mixture, starting and finishing with the flour. Stir in vanilla. Distribute the batter evenly among prepared muffin cups.
- *For the frosting*, beat together cream cheese, tofu and sugar until fluffy, then beat in egg.
- Top each cupcake with the frosting and press with 3 M&Ms® (or Smarties®) into the center (these may slide down somewhat as they bake). Bake for 20 minutes. Cool on wire rack.

makes 24 medium cupcakes
preparation time: 25 minutes
baking time: 20 minutes

PER CUPCAKE: 143 calories, 4 g protein, 19 g carbohydrate, 6 g total fat (3 g sat fat, 2 g mono fat, 1 g poly fat), 26 mg cholesterol, 1 g dietary fiber, 46 RE vitamin A, 3 mcg folate, < .5 vitamin C, 11 g calcium, 1 mg iron, 81 mg potassium, 109 mg sodium

cocoa layer cake
with chocolate cream frosting

THE PERFECT birthday cake for a chocolate lover: chocolate cake *and* chocolate frosting with only five grams of saturated fat per serving!

¹/₂ cup	unsweetened cocoa powder	125 mL
¹/₂ cup	boiling water	125 mL
1³/₄ cups	unbleached flour	425 mL
2 tbsp.	soy flour	30 mL
1 tsp.	baking powder	5 mL
1 tsp.	baking soda	5 mL
	pinch of salt	
¹/₄ cup	butter or margarine, softened	60 mL
¹/₄ cup	soft tofu	60 mL
1¹/₂ cups	sugar	375 mL
2	eggs	2
1 tsp.	vanilla extract	5 mL
1¹/₃ cups	soy milk	325 mL
	Chocolate Cream Frosting, below	

- Preheat oven to 350° F (180° C). Grease two 9-inch (23 cm) round cake pans.
- In a small bowl, combine cocoa and boiling water; set aside and let cool.
- In another small bowl, sift together flours, baking powder, baking soda, and salt.
- In a large bowl, using an electric mixer or hand blender, beat butter, tofu, sugar, eggs, and vanilla until fluffy. Then blend in flour mixture and soy milk alternately in four parts until batter is smooth.
- Stir cooled cocoa mixture into batter. Divide evenly between the two pans. Bake 30 minutes, or until a toothpick inserted in center comes out clean. Let stand 10 minutes, then remove from pans. Cool completely.
- To assemble cake, place one cake on a serving plate and spread ¹/₄ of the frosting over it. Place other cake on top and spread the remaining frosting over the top and sides of cake. For best results, assemble cake shortly before serving (up to 2 hours); chill until ready to serve.

chocolate cream frosting

¾ cup	whipping cream	175 mL
4 oz.	soy cream cheese	125 g
½ cup	soft tofu	125 mL
¼ cup	granulated sugar	60 mL
2 tbsp.	unsweetened cocoa	30 mL
1 tsp.	vanilla extract	5 mL

- In a medium bowl, whip cream.
- In a large bowl, using the same beaters, beat remaining ingredients until smooth. Fold in whipped cream. Cover and chill until ready to frost cake.

makes 16 servings
preparation time: 40 minutes
cooking time: 30 minutes

PER SERVING: 246 calories, 5 g protein, 35 g carbohydrate, 11 g total fat (5 g sat fat, 2 g mono fat, 2 g poly fat), 46 mg cholesterol, 2 g dietary fiber, 89 RE vitamin A, 4 mcg folate, < .5 vitamin C, 20 mg calcium, 2 mg iron, 121 mg potassium, 119 mg sodium

sour cream chocolate cake

TOFU AND soy flour replace two egg yolks in this scrumptious cake, which guests devour every time Bettina makes it.

1 1/2 cups	unbleached flour	375 mL
1/2 cup	soy flour	125 mL
3/4 cup	unsweetened cocoa powder, sifted	175 mL
2 tsp.	baking powder	10 mL
1 tsp.	baking soda	5 mL
1/2 tsp.	salt	2 mL
1 cup	granulated sugar	250 mL
1/2 cup	butter or margarine, softened	125 mL
1/4 cup	soft tofu	60 mL
1	egg	1
2	egg whites	2
1 1/4 cups	soy milk	310 mL
1 tsp.	vanilla extract	5 mL

frosting

1/3 cup	unsweetened cocoa	75 mL
1/3 cup	sugar	75 mL
1 cup	soy sour cream	250 mL
1 cup	soft tofu	250 mL

- Preheat oven to 350° F (180° C). Grease two 9-inch (23 cm) cake pans.
- In a medium bowl, mix together flours, cocoa, baking powder, baking soda, and salt.
- In large bowl, using an electric mixer or hand blender, beat sugar, butter, and tofu until fluffy. Beat in egg and egg whites, until well combined.
- Alternately beat flour mixture and soy milk into the creamy mixture, starting and finishing with the flour. Stir in vanilla.
- Divide the batter evenly between the two pans and bake for 25 to 30 minutes, or until a toothpick inserted in center comes out clean. Cool for 10 minutes, then remove and cool completely on wire rack.
- *For the frosting*, beat all ingredients together until well combined and smooth.
- To assemble cake, place one cake on a serving plate and spread ¼ of the frosting over it. Place other cake on top and spread the remaining frosting over the top and sides of cake. For best results, assemble cake shortly before serving (up to 2 hours); chill until ready to serve.

makes 16 servings
preparation time: 25 minutes
baking time: 25–30 minutes

PER SERVING: 227 calories, 7 g protein, 30 g carbohydrate, 10 g total fat (5 g sat fat, 2 g mono fat, 2 g poly fat), 27 mg cholesterol, 3 g dietary fiber, 66 RE vitamin A, 4 mcg folate, < .5 vitamin C, 18 mg calcium, 2 mg iron, 167 mg potassium, 238 mg sodium

chocolate cream puffs
with grand marnier cream filling

FOR A festive occasion, cream puffs look stunning on a dessert table. My daughter Bettina makes pyramid centerpieces of cream-filled miniature puffs, all held together by caramelized sugar—a tantalizing showpiece for the eyes and treat for the tastebuds.

Puffs can be made a day ahead, then filled with cream a few hours before serving.

grand marnier cream filling

½ cup	whipping cream	125 mL
4 oz.	soy cream cheese	125 g
½ cup	soft tofu	125 mL
¼ cup	granulated sugar	60 mL
2 tsp.	grated orange peel	10 mL
1–2 tsp.	orange juice	5–10 mL
1 tbsp.	Grand Marnier or orange brandy	15 mL

chocolate puff pastry

3	large eggs	3
1 tbsp.	soy milk	15 mL
¾ cup	unbleached flour	175 mL
2 tbsp.	soy flour	30 mL
2 tbsp.	unsweetened cocoa powder	30 mL
1 tbsp.	granulated sugar	15 mL
	pinch of salt	
1 cup	water	250 mL
6 tbsp.	butter or margarine, cut up	90 mL
	confectioner's sugar, for sprinkling (optional)	

- *To make the filling*, whip cream in a medium bowl.
- In a separate bowl, using the same beaters, gradually beat together remaining ingredients until smooth. Fold in whipped cream. Cover and chill until ready to fill puffs.
- *To make the puff pastry*, blend eggs and soy milk, using an electric hand blender. Set aside.
- In a small bowl, combine flours, cocoa, sugar, and salt.
- In a medium nonstick saucepan, bring water and butter to a boil. Add flour mixture, stirring vigorously until mixture leaves sides of pan and forms a smooth ball. Remove from heat. Gradually beat in egg mixture until smooth. Spoon dough into 12 to 14 mounds onto ungreased baking sheet, about 3 inches (7.5 cm) apart.
- Bake in 400° F (200° C) oven for about 35 minutes, or until puffed and edges start to brown. Poke holes in sides with a toothpick to release steam. Cool on wire rack.
- Cut tops off puffs. Fill bottoms generously with cream filling. Replace tops and dust with confectioner's sugar, if desired. Cover and chill until ready to serve. Best when served same day.

makes 12–14 cream puffs
preparation time: cream filling, 10 minutes
puff pastry, 10 minutes
assembly, 10 minutes
baking time: 35 minutes

PER CREAM PUFF: 160 calories, 4 g protein, 11 g carbohydrate, 11 g total fat (6 g sat fat, 3 g mono fat, 2 g poly fat), 68 mg cholesterol, 1 g dietary fiber, 95 RE vitamin A, 6 mcg folate, 1 mg vitamin C, 17 mg calcium, 1 mg iron, 79 mg potassium, 57 mg sodium

chocolate raspberry pavlova

MERINGUES ARE among my favorite desserts, especially when served with cream and berries. This luscious chocolate version makes an especially festive end to a meal.

meringue

6	egg whites	6
	pinch of salt	
¼ tsp.	cream of tartar	1 mL
1½ cups	granulated sugar	375 mL
2 tbsp.	unsweetened cocoa powder	30 mL
2 tsp.	cornstarch	10 mL
1 tbsp.	vinegar	15 mL
1 tsp.	vanilla extract	5 mL
1 tbsp.	crushed honey-roasted soynuts	15 mL

topping

	Best Whipped Topping, page 170	
3 cups	fresh raspberries	750 mL
1 oz.	semisweet chocolate, melted (optional)	28 g

- Preheat oven to 275° F (140° C).
- Line a cookie sheet with parchment paper. Draw an 8-inch (20 cm) circle on it.
- In a large bowl, beat together egg whites, salt, and cream of tartar until soft peaks form. Gradually beat in sugar until whites are stiff. Sift cocoa and cornstarch over whites, then fold in gently. Fold in vinegar, vanilla, and crushed soynuts. Mound egg white mixture onto circle on cookie sheet, flattening the top slightly with a spatula.
- Bake in center of oven for 1½ hours, or until crisp on the outside but still soft in the center. Loosen meringue with a spatula and transfer to wire rack. Cool completely.
- Shortly before serving, place meringue on a serving platter. Spread Best Whipped Topping over it. Top with raspberries. Drizzle melted chocolate over raspberries, if desired.

makes 6 to 8 servings
preparation time: meringue, 15 minutes
topping, 15 minutes
baking time: 1½ hours

PER SERVING: 266 calories, 5 g protein, 48 g carbohydrate, 6 g total fat (4 g sat fat, 2 g mono fat, < .5 g poly fat), 20 mg cholesterol, 1 g dietary fiber, 64 RE vitamin A, 2 mcg folate, 1 mg vitamin C, 20 mg calcium, 1 mg iron, 96 mg potassium, 69 mg sodium

ultra light cheesecake

THIS CRUSTLESS make-ahead cake takes a fraction of the time needed to make most baked cheesecakes. Dress it up with your favorite berries or sauce and you've got a delicious light dessert.

4 oz.	soy cream cheese	125 g
1 cup	soft tofu	250 mL
8 oz.	light ricotta cheese	250 g
½ cup	granulated sugar	125 mL
2	eggs*	2
1½ tbsp.	cornstarch	22 mL
1½ tbsp.	soy flour	22 mL
2 tsp.	lemon juice	10 mL
½ tsp.	vanilla extract	2 mL
½ cup	light sour cream	125 mL
2 tbsp.	butter or margarine, melted	30 mL

- Preheat oven to 325° F (165° C).
- In a large bowl, using an electric mixer or hand blender, blend together cream cheese, tofu, and ricotta cheese until creamy. Gradually add sugar and eggs. Beat in remaining ingredients until smooth.
- Pour into a lightly greased 8-inch (20 cm) springform pan and bake for 50 to 60 minutes, or until edges are firm but center is still soft. Turn off heat and let cake stand in oven for 2 hours. Chill at least 4 hours or overnight.
- Serve cake with puréed berries.

makes 8 servings
preparation time: 15 minutes
baking time: 50–60 minutes
standing time: 2 hours
chilling time: 4 hours

*Liquid egg substitute works well in this recipe. Substitute ⅓ to ⅔ cup (about 100 mL) liquid egg for the 2 eggs.

PER SERVING: 138 calories, 5 g protein, 13 g carbohydrate, 7 g total fat (3 g sat fat, 1 g mono fat, 2 g poly fat), 43 mg cholesterol, < .5 g dietary fiber, 46 RE vitamin A, 4 mcg folate, < .5 mg vitamin C, 42 mg calcium, < .5 mg iron, 79 mg potassium, 85 mg sodium

cheesecake with swirled lemon curd

Tangy lemon curd swirled into a combination of soy cream cheese, ricotta cheese, and tofu makes this the ultimate cheesecake. Low in saturated fats, this cake rivals any you've ever had for flavor and texture.

crust

½ cup	unbleached flour	125 mL
¼ cup	soy flour	60 mL
2 tbsp.	granulated sugar	30 mL
2 tbsp.	cold butter	30 mL
2 tbsp.	ice water	30 mL

filling

16 oz.	soy cream cheese	500 g
8 oz.	light ricotta cheese	250 g
1 cup	soft tofu	250 mL
1½ cups	granulated sugar	375 mL
3 tbsp.	soy flour	45 mL
1 tbsp.	grated lemon peel	15 mL
2 tsp.	vanilla extract	10 mL
¼ tsp.	salt	1 mL
4	large eggs	4
½ cup	Lemon Curd, page 174	125 mL

- Make Lemon Curd. Set aside.
- *To make the crust*, combine flours and sugar in a medium bowl. With a pastry blender, cut in butter until mixture resembles coarse crumbs. Stir in water and, while still crumbly, press mixture into the bottom of a greased 10-inch (25 cm) springform pan. Bake at 400° F (200° C) for 10 minutes, then cool on wire rack while preparing the filling.
- Reduce oven temperature to 325° F (165° C).

- *To make the filling*, use an electric mixer to beat cream cheese, ricotta cheese, and tofu until smooth. Gradually beat in sugar, flour, lemon peel, vanilla, salt, and eggs. Pour mixture into pan over partially baked crust.
- Spoon ½ of lemon curd over filling and swirl with a knife.
- Bake 1 hour 20 minutes, or until cheesecake is almost set (there will be cracks around the edge of the cake). Remove cake from oven and cool to room temperature. Cover and chill for at least 8 hours or overnight.
- Serve cake with dollops of remaining lemon curd on the side, if desired.

makes 14–16 servings
preparation time: cake, 40 minutes
                          lemon curd, 10 minutes
baking time: 1 hour 20 minutes
chilling time: 8 hours to overnight

PER SERVING: 256 calories, 7 g protein, 31 g carbohydrate, 12 g total fat (4 g sat fat, 1 g mono fat, 6 g poly fat), 71 mg cholesterol, < .5 g dietary fiber, 61 RE vitamin A, 8 mcg folate, 3 mg vitamin C, 37 mg calcium, 1 mg iron, 59 mg potassium, 206 mg sodium

cream cheese, tofu, and mocha cake
non-dairy

LUSCIOUSLY MOIST with its "baked-in" tofu and soy cream cheese filling, this attractive and delicious cake, topped with an exquisite mocha frosting, was gobbled up by my taste testers who gave it rave reviews.

	Cream Cheese and Tofu Filling (below)	
⅓ cup	butter or margarine, softened	75 mL
1 cup	packed brown sugar	250 mL
1	egg	1
1 cup	soy milk	250 mL
½ cup	water	125 mL
1½ cups	unbleached flour	375 mL
¼ cup	whole wheat flour	60 mL
¼ cup	soy flour	60 mL
¼ tsp. each	ground cinnamon and cloves	1 mL
1¼ tsp.	baking powder	6 mL
1 tsp.	baking soda	5 mL
¼–½ cup	chopped nuts	60–125 mL
	Mocha Frosting (below)	

- Preheat oven to 350° F (180° C). Lightly grease a 9 x 13-inch (23 x 33 cm) baking dish.
- Make Cream Cheese and Tofu Filling.
- In a large bowl, beat together butter, sugar, egg, soy milk, and water. Gradually stir in remaining ingredients (except Mocha Frosting). Spread half of batter in prepared baking dish. Spoon filling over batter. Spread remaining batter over filling.
- Bake 40 to 45 minutes, or until toothpick inserted in center comes out clean. When cool, spread Mocha Frosting over top of cake.

4 oz.	soy cream cheese	125 g
½ cup	soft tofu	125 mL
¼ cup	granulated sugar	60 mL
1	egg white	1
½ tsp.	vanilla extract	2 mL

- In a medium bowl, mix all ingredients with a fork until smooth.

1 tbsp.	hot water	15 mL
½ tsp.	instant coffee granules	2 mL
½ tsp.	ground cinnamon	2 mL
1 tbsp.	unsweetened cocoa	15 mL
2 cups	icing sugar	500 mL
2 tbsp.	butter or margarine, softened	30 mL
2 tbsp.	soft tofu	30 mL

- In a medium bowl, combine hot water, coffee, cinnamon, and cocoa. Beat in remaining ingredients until smooth.

makes 18 servings
preparation time: 30 minutes
baking time: 40–45 minutes

PER SERVING: 240 calories, 4 g protein, 38 g carbohydrate, 8 g total fat (4 g sat fat, 2 g mono fat, 2 g poly fat), 23 mg cholesterol, 1 g dietary fiber, 52 RE vitamin A, 3 mcg folate, < .5 mg vitamin C, 19 mg calcium, 1 mg iron, 111 mg potassium, 142 mg sodium

cakes & frostings

mocha cinnamon torte

THIS SPECTACULAR cake consists of luscious mocha cream sandwiched between four thin layers of giant cinnamon cookies. The filling, although high in calories, is greatly reduced in saturated fats by the substitution of cholesterol-free cream cheese and tofu for regular cream cheese. It's a treat, so enjoy!

½ cup	butter or margarine, softened	125 mL
2 tbsp.	soybean oil	30 mL
1 cup	granulated sugar	250 mL
2	eggs	2
1	egg white	1
1½ cups	unbleached flour	375 mL
½ cup	soy flour	125 mL
1 tbsp.	ground cinnamon	15 mL
2½ tsp.	baking powder	12 mL
¼ tsp.	salt	1 mL

filling

1 tsp.	instant coffee granules	5 mL
1 tsp.	vanilla extract	5 mL
1 cup	soy sour cream	250 mL
1 cup	soft tofu	250 mL
¾ cup	granulated sugar	175 mL
½ cup	unsweetened cocoa powder	125 mL
1 cup	whipping cream	250 mL

- Preheat oven to 350° F (180° C). Line two cookie sheets with parchment paper. Draw two 9-inch (23 cm) circles on each.
- In a medium bowl, using an electric mixer or hand blender, beat butter, oil, and sugar until fluffy. Beat in eggs and egg white. Gradually mix in flours, cinnamon, baking powder, and salt.
- Divide batter evenly among the four circles on cookie sheets. Spread very thinly with a knife to fill in circles. Bake, one sheet at a time, in center of oven, for 15 to 18 minutes, or until just starting to brown around the edges. Let cool on sheet on wire rack.

- *To make the filling*, combine coffee granules and vanilla in a small bowl.
- In a medium bowl, using an electric mixer or hand blender, blend together sour cream, tofu, sugar, and cocoa; blend in coffee mixture.
- In a large bowl, whip cream; fold into sour cream mixture. Cover and chill until ready to assemble torte.
- Place cookie layers on work surface. Spread about ¼ of filling evenly over each layer; stack layers. Make swirls on top layer and garnish with chocolate shavings or curls, if desired. Chill at least 4 hours to let flavors blend.
- *To make chocolate shavings or curls*, chill chocolate for easier handling. Using a grater to make shavings, grate chocolate onto a piece of waxed paper. Try different sizes on grater to get the desired shape. For chocolate curls, scrape chocolate onto waxed paper with a sharp-edged table peeler. Chill chocolate shavings and curls until ready to use.

makes 12 servings
preparation time: cookie layers, 20 minutes
filling, 15 minutes
assembly, 10 minutes
baking time: about 18 minutes per batch

VARIATIONS: Different cream fillings such as Orange Cream, page 176, Margarita Dip, page 179 or Best Whipped Topping, page 170, also go well with the cinnamon cookie layers.

PER SERVING: 403 calories, 8 g protein, 46 g carbohydrate, 23 g total fat (12 g sat fat, 5 g mono fat, 3 g poly fat), 79 mg cholesterol, 2 g dietary fiber, 178 RE vitamin A, 6 mcg folate, < .5 vitamin C, 38 mg calcium, 2 mg iron, 133 mg potassium, 215 mg sodium

tiramisu

ALTHOUGH THIS won't win the prize for lowest calories, this much-loved dessert is perfect for special occasions. Making it a day ahead of your dinner party gives the flavors time to meld—and frees you up to enjoy time with your guests.

	Amaretto or other liqueur, to taste	
	Espresso coffee (enough to soak cookies, about 2 cups)	
16 oz.	soy cream cheese (*or* 8 oz. soy cream cheese + 8 oz. mascarpone cheese*)	500 g
¼ cup	granulated sugar	60 mL
1 tsp.	vanilla extract	5 mL
2	eggs, separated	2
1	egg white	1
1 lb. pkg.	Savoiardi cookies (Ladyfingers)	400 g
2 tbsp.	crushed roasted soynuts, optional	30 mL
	cocoa for sprinkling, optional	

- Add liqueur to coffee. Set aside.
- In a medium bowl, using an electric mixer or hand blender, blend together soy cream cheese, sugar, vanilla, and egg yolks until smooth.
- In a separate bowl, beat egg whites until stiff. Fold into creamed mixture.
- Dip cookies into coffee liqueur and cover bottom of a large rectangular or oval serving platter with ⅓ of cookies (about 20). Spread ⅓ of creamed mixture over cookies. Continue layering, ending with the creamed mixture. Cover and chill at least 4 hours or overnight.
- Just before serving, sprinkle with soynuts and cocoa, if desired.

makes 8–10 servings
preparation time: 30 minutes
chilling time: 4 hours to overnight

*For a more authentic Tiramisu flavor, use half mascarpone, half soy cream cheese.

PER SERVING: 344 calories, 9 g protein, 35 g carbohydrate, 18 g total fat (5 g sat fat, 2 g mono fat, 10 g poly fat), 203 mg cholesterol, 1 g dietary fiber, 109 RE vitamin A, 40 mcg folate, 2 mg vitamin C, 32 mg calcium, 2 mg iron, 120 mg potassium, 329 mg sodium

AN EASY to make cake that looks and tastes wonderful. Moist, tangy, and light.

²/₃ cup	granulated sugar, divided	150 mL
¹/₂ cup	fresh lemon juice, divided	125 mL
¹/₄ cup	butter or margarine, softened	60 mL
¹/₄ cup	soft tofu	60 mL
1	egg	1
2	egg whites	2
¹/₃ cup	soy milk	75 mL
1¹/₂ cups	unbleached flour	375 mL
2 tbsp.	soy flour	30 mL
1 tbsp.	baking powder	15 mL
¹/₄ tsp.	salt	1 mL
1 cup	confectioner's sugar, for the frosting	250 mL
1 tbsp.	toasted soy flakes (optional)	15 mL
2 tbsp.	finely shredded lemon peel	30 mL

- Preheat oven to 350° F (180° C). Grease an 8-inch (20 cm) round cake pan.
- *For the lemon glaze,* combine ¹/₃ cup (75 mL) granulated sugar with all but 2 tbsp. (30 mL) of the lemon juice. Set aside.
- In a large bowl, using an electric mixer or hand blender, blend together butter, tofu, and remaining ¹/₃ cup (75 mL) granulated sugar. Beat in egg, egg whites, and soy milk. Gradually stir in flours, baking powder, and salt to form a thick, smooth batter.
- Spread batter in prepared pan and bake 45 to 50 minutes, or until toothpick inserted in center comes out clean.
- With a toothpick, poke 15 to 20 holes in top of cake. Spoon lemon glaze over it. Cool cake completely before transferring it to a serving platter.
- *To make the icing,* combine confectioner's sugar with only as much of the reserved 2 tbsp. (30 mL) lemon juice as needed to make it spreadable. Spoon over cake, letting it drip over the edge. Sprinkle with soy flakes, if using, and shredded lemon peel.

makes 8 to 10 servings
preparation time: 25 minutes
baking time: 45–50 minutes
freezes well

PER SERVING: 226 calories, 4 g protein, 40 g carbohydrate, 5 g total fat (3 g sat fat, 2 g mono fat, < .5 g poly fat), 31 mg cholesterol, 1 g dietary fiber, 52 RE vitamin A, 4 mcg folate, 7 mg vitamin C, 9 mg calcium, 1 mg iron, 57 mg potassium, 164 mg sodium

pineapple upside down cake

MY FRIENDS and neighbors Bruce and Joanne York have been among my primary taste testers while I was developing the recipes for this book. Joanne created this deliciously moist cake recipe from a more traditional version.

¼ cup	maple syrup	60 mL
14 oz. can	pineapple rings, drained	398 mL
7 or 8	maraschino cherries	7 or 8
¾ cup	unbleached flour	175 mL
¼ cup	soy flour	60 mL
1 tsp.	baking powder	5 mL
¼ tsp.	baking soda	1 mL
¼ tsp.	ground cinnamon	1 mL
¼ tsp.	salt	1 mL
½ cup	granulated sugar	125 mL
¼ cup	butter or margarine, softened	60 mL
1	large egg	1
1	egg white	1
½ cup	vanilla soy milk	125 mL
1 tbsp.	lemon juice	15 mL

- In a 10-inch (25 cm) nonstick or cast-iron skillet, over medium heat, bring maple syrup to a boil. Remove from heat. Arrange pineapple slices in skillet with one in the center and the others in a wagon wheel around it. Garnish with cherries, pitted side up.
- Place pan over medium heat and cook until syrup thickens, about 4 minutes, frequently shaking the pan to prevent sticking and burning.
- In a medium bowl, combine flours, baking powder, baking soda, cinnamon, and salt.
- In a separate bowl, using an electric mixer or hand blender, beat sugar and butter until smooth. Add egg, egg white, soy milk, and lemon juice. Gradually beat in flour mixture.
- Pour batter evenly over pineapple rings. Wrap handle of skillet with foil.
- Bake at 350° F (180° C) for 30 minutes, or until cake springs back when touched lightly in center. Run knife around edge to loosen cake. Cool in pan 5 minutes. Place a serving platter upside down on top of cake; invert to unmold cake. Serve warm or at room temperature.

makes 8 or 9 servings
preparation time: 20 minutes
baking time: 30 minutes
freezes well

PER SERVING: 200 calories, 4 g protein, 34 g carbohydrate, 6 g total fat (3 g sat fat, 2 g mono fat, < .5 g poly fat), 37 mg cholesterol, 1 g dietary fiber, 60 RE vitamin A, 6 mcg folate, 4 mg vitamin C, 19 mg calcium, 1 mg iron, 110 mg potassium, 138 mg sodium

pies & tarts

basic shortbread crust

THIS NUTTY flavored soy crust is an easy-to-make and versatile base for squares, bars, and pies—use it wherever a more traditional shortbread crust is called for.

1 cup	unbleached flour	250 mL
¼ cup	soy flour	60 mL
	pinch of salt	
3 tbsp.	cold butter, cubed	45 mL
2 tbsp.	roasted soy flakes	30 mL
½ tsp.	vanilla extract	2 mL
1–2 tbsp.	soy milk	15–30 mL

- Grease a 9-inch (23 cm) square cake pan.
- In a food processor or with a pastry blender, blend flours, salt, and butter until mixture resembles coarse crumbs. Sprinkle soy flakes, vanilla, and soy milk over mixture and work in until evenly distributed. Press into bottom of cake pan.
- Bake according to pie/square recipe directions.

makes one 9-inch (23 cm) square crust;
9–12 servings
preparation time: 15 minutes
baking time: with filling, 30–40 minutes

PER SERVING: 79 calories, 3 g protein, 9 g carbohydrate, 4 g total fat (2 g sat fat, 1 g mono fat, < .5 g poly fat), 8 mg cholesterol, < .5 g dietary fiber, 27 RE vitamin A, < .5 mcg folate, 1 mg calcium, < .5 mg iron, 3 mg potassium, 1 mg sodium

pastry crust for fruit pies and tarts

I ENJOY this light buttery crust and use it often for fruit pies and tarts. Try it when you make Lemon-Lime Tart, page 77.

page 77

one 9-inch crust

½ cup	unbleached flour	125 mL
¼ cup	soy flour	60 mL
2 tbsp.	toasted soy flakes	30 mL
1 tbsp.	confectioner's sugar	15 mL
½ tsp.	baking powder	2 mL
	pinch of salt	
¼ cup	cold butter or margarine	60 mL
1	egg yolk, chilled	1
¼ cup	cold water	60 mL

- In a food processor or with a pastry blender, blend flours, soy flakes, sugar, baking powder, salt, and butter until mixture resembles coarse crumbs. Quickly work in egg yolk and cold water until mixture holds together. Gather into a ball, cover and chill 30 minutes or until ready to use.
- Roll out dough on floured surface to fit a 9-inch pie plate. Fill and bake according to pie/tart recipe directions.★

makes one 9-inch (14 cm) pie crust, 8 servings
preparation time: 15 minutes

*To bake an unfilled pie shell, line pie plate with pastry; place a sheet of heavy aluminum foil over the pastry, shiny side down. Smooth foil over pastry bottom and let foil edges shield the crust edge. Use raw rice or beans to weigh down the foil. Bake crust at 400° F (200° C) for 20 minutes. Remove rice or beans and foil. With a fork, prick the crust all over and bake 5 to 10 minutes more, until golden.

PER SERVING: 116 calories, 5 g protein, 9 g carbohydrate, 7 g total fat (4 g sat fat, 2 g mono fat, < .5 g poly fat), 42 mg cholesterol, 1 g dietary fiber, 66 RE vitamin A, 3 mcg folate, 5 mg calcium, 1 mg iron, 4 mg potassium, 28 mg sodium

flan pastry crust
non-dairy, 1-bowl recipe

AN ALL-PURPOSE lightly sweetened crust for fruit pies. Although defatted soy flour works well, stone-ground whole-grain soy flour enhances this crust with an earthy, nutty flavor.

²/₃ cup	unbleached flour	150 mL
¹/₃ cup	whole wheat flour	75 mL
¹/₃ cup	soy flour	75 mL
¹/₄ cup	packed brown sugar	60 mL
¹/₄ tsp.	baking powder	1 mL
1 tsp.	grated lemon peel	5 mL
¹/₂ cup	butter or margarine, softened	125 mL
¹/₄ cup	soft tofu	60 mL

- In a medium bowl, mix all ingredients until crumbly. Press firmly and evenly against bottom and edge of an ungreased 12-inch pizza pan. Bake according to flan/pie recipe directions.

makes 8 servings
preparation time: 15 minutes
baking time: 30 minutes with a fruit filling
freezes well

PER SERVING: 198 calories, 5 g protein, 19 g carbohydrate, 12 g total fat (7 g sat fat, 3 g mono fat, < .5 g poly fat), 31 mg cholesterol, 1 g dietary fiber, 108 RE vitamin A, 1 mcg folate, < .5 mg vitamin C, 12 mg calcium, 1 mg iron, 44 mg potassium, 19 mg sodium

graham cracker crust

THE TOASTED soy flakes add a nutty flavor to this popular and versatile crust. It's the perfect base for Key Lime Pie (page 68).

1 cup	graham cracker crumbs	250 mL
¼ cup	toasted soy flakes	60 mL
¼ cup	granulated sugar	60 mL
¼ cup	butter or margarine, melted	60 mL

- Preheat oven to 325° F (165° C).
- In a medium bowl, combine crumbs, soy flakes, and sugar. Stir in melted butter. Press onto bottom and sides of a 9-inch (23 cm) pie plate. Bake 5 to 10 minutes.

makes one 9-inch (23 cm) pie crust
preparation time: 10 minutes
baking time: 5–10 minutes

PER SERVING: 181 calories, 4 g protein, 19 g carbohydrate, 10 g total fat (4 g sat fat, 2 g mono fat, < .5 g poly fat), 16 mg cholesterol, 2 g dietary fiber, 53 RE vitamin A, < .5 mcg folate, 4 mg calcium, < .5 mg iron, 23 mg potassium, 61 mg sodium

apple pie
non-dairy

SIMPLE COMFORT food at its best! This easy-to-make crust is suitable for all fruit pies.

sweet pastry crust

¾ cup	unbleached flour	175 mL
¼ cup	soy flour	60 mL
¼ cup	sugar	60 mL
	pinch of salt	
1 tsp.	baking powder	5 mL
½ cup	butter or margarine, chilled	125 mL
1	egg, beaten	1

filling

1–2 tbsp.	raisins	15–30 mL
3 tbsp.	brandy	45 mL
3–4	medium apples	3–4
6 tbsp.	vanilla soy milk, divided	90 mL
2 tsp.	soy or wheat flour	10 mL
2 tbsp.	sugar (add more, if apples are tart)	30 mL
1–2 tbsp.	ground hazelnuts or soynuts (optional)	15–30 mL

- *To make the pastry,* sift together flours, sugar, salt, and baking powder into a medium bowl. Mix butter into flour with a pastry blender until mixture resembles coarse crumbs. Work in egg until dough holds together. Press ¾ of dough firmly and evenly against bottom and side of an ungreased nonstick 9-inch (23 cm) pie plate. On a floured surface, roll out remaining dough to ¼-inch (.6 cm) thickness and cut out different shapes with a cookie cutter (stars look great).
- *For the filling,* soak raisins in brandy.
- Peel, core, halve, and thinly slice the apples. Arrange apple slices in pie shell.
- Add 4 tbsp. (60 mL) of the vanilla soy milk and flour to raisins and spoon mixture evenly over apples. Sprinkle with 1½ tbsp. (22 mL) sugar and hazelnuts or soynuts, if using. Decorate top with cut-out dough. Brush cut-outs with remaining soy milk and sprinkle with a little more sugar.
- Bake at 350° F (180° C) for 40 to 45 minutes, or until crust is golden and apples are soft.

makes one 9-inch (23 cm) pie, 8 servings
preparation time: pastry, 15 minutes; filling, 15 minutes
baking time: 40–45 minutes
dough freezes well
baked pie freezes well

PER SERVING (PIE CRUST ONLY): 182 calories, 4 g protein, 15 g carbohydrate, 12 g total fat (7 g sat fat, 4 g mono fat, 1 g poly fat), 54 mg cholesterol, < .5 g dietary fiber, 117 RE vitamin A, 3 mcg folate, 6 mg calcium, 1 mg iron, 10 mg potassium, 60 mg sodium

PER SERVING (APPLE PIE): 234 calories, 5 g protein, 25 g carbohydrate, 12 g total fat (7 g sat fat, 4 g mono fat, 1 g poly fat), 54 mg cholesterol, 2 g dietary fiber, 120 RE vitamin A, 10 mcg folate, 3 mg vitamin C, 11 mg calcium, 1 mg iron, 96 mg potassium, 62 mg sodium

plum pie
non-dairy

MY MOTHER Ruth Stolz has been an avid baker all her life, her specialties being yeast breads and fruit pies. At age 80 she is still "baking up a storm," baking half a dozen pies in one day, then freezing them as needed. Plum pie is the family favorite as much as ever with the addition of soy flakes.

9-inch	single Sweet Pastry Crust, page 64	23 cm
2 tbsp.	toasted soy flakes, divided	30 mL
1 lb.	ripe Italian plums, quartered	500 g
2 tbsp.	bread crumbs	30 mL
1–2 tbsp.	brown sugar (add more, if plums are tart)	15–30 mL
1 tbsp.	dark rum	15 mL
2 tsp.	butter or margarine	10 mL

- Preheat oven to 350° F (180° C).
- Make pie crust and line a greased pie plate with it. Sprinkle bottom with one tbsp. (15 mL) soy flakes. Arrange quartered plums tightly in a circular pattern on pastry.
- In a small bowl, combine bread crumbs, sugar, remaining one tbsp. (15 mL) soy flakes, and rum. Sprinkle over plums. Dot with butter.
- Bake 40 to 45 minutes, or until plums are soft and juicy and crust is golden. Cool on wire rack and serve with Best Whipped Topping, page 170, if desired.

makes 8 servings
preparation time: crust, 15 minutes
fruit topping, 15 minutes
baking time: 40–45 minutes
freezes well

PER SERVING: 251 calories, 6 g protein, 26 g carbohydrate, 14 g total fat (8 g sat fat, 4 g mono fat, 1 g poly fat), 57 mg cholesterol, 2 g dietary fiber, 145 RE vitamin A, 5 mcg folate, 5 mg vitamin C, 10 mg calcium, 1 mg iron, 113 mg potassium, 71 mg sodium

NOTE: Italian plums which are small, oval, and bluish-purple in color, are my personal preference. Feel free to substitute your own favorite type of plum.

the soy dessert & baking book

PEACH SEASON never lasts long enough for me. I live near Niagara Falls where it lasts little more than a month. So, while peaches are fresh and readily available, I find ways to add them to all my cooking and baking, from salads and stir-fries to desserts like this mouthwatering pie.

9-inch	single unbaked Pastry Crust for Fruit Pies and Tarts, page 61	23 cm
4	ripe peaches, peeled and sliced	4
1/2 cup	soft tofu	125 mL
1/4 cup	soy sour cream	60 mL
2 tbsp.	frozen orange juice concentrate	30 mL
3–4 tbsp.	granulated sugar	45–60 mL
2 tsp.	soy or wheat flour	10 mL
1/4 cup	vanilla soy milk	60 mL
1 tbsp.	sliced almonds	15 mL
1 tbsp.	brown sugar	15 mL

- Line bottom and sides of pie plate with pastry.
- Preheat oven to 375° F (180° C).
- Arrange peach slices on pastry, overlapping slightly, starting at the outside and working toward the center.
- In a medium bowl, using an electric mixer or hand blender, blend together tofu, sour cream, orange juice, sugar, flour, and soy milk until smooth and creamy. Spoon over peaches. Sprinkle with almonds and brown sugar.
- Bake 35 to 40 minutes, or until crust is golden and filling is set. Cool to room temperature.

makes 8 servings
preparation time: crust, 15 minutes
                    filling, 15 minutes
baking time: 35–40 minutes

VARIATIONS: Instead of peaches, try apricots, apples, or pears.

PER SERVING: 197 calories, 7 g protein, 23 g carbohydrate,10 g total fat (4 g sat fat, 2 g mono fat, 1 g poly fat), 42 mg cholesterol, 2 g dietary fiber, 98 RE vitamin A, 12 mcg folate, 9 mg vitamin C, 17 mg calcium, 1 mg iron, 182 mg potassium, 61 mg sodium

key lime pie

MY YEARLY visits to Florida would not be complete without indulging in this most flavorful of pies. I have substituted tofu and soy milk for one egg, one egg yolk, and half the cream called for in the original recipe. The result is a light fluffy filling. Note that key limes are smaller and have a more subtle flavor than regular limes, but if you can't find key limes (which, outside of Florida are typically found in specialty grocers) regular limes will work, as well.

2 tbsp.	toasted sliced almonds	30 mL
9-inch	Graham Cracker Crust, page 63	23 cm
1 tbsp.	(1 packet) unflavored gelatin	15 mL
1 cup	granulated sugar, divided	250 mL
	pinch of salt	
2	large eggs, separated	2
1/4 cup	soy milk	60 mL
1/2 cup	fresh lime juice, strained	125 mL
1 tsp.	grated lime peel	5 mL
1/2 cup	whipping cream	125 mL
1/2 cup	soft tofu	125 mL
4	thin slices of lime, cut in half, as a garnish	4
	Best Whipped Topping, page 170, as a garnish (optional)	

- Sprinkle almonds evenly over base of pie crust.
- In a small saucepan, combine gelatin, 1/2 cup (125 mL) sugar, and salt.
- In a separate bowl, beat egg yolks with soy milk; stir in lime juice. Pour into gelatin mixture. Cook over low heat, stirring constantly, just until mixture is thickened and smooth. Remove from heat, then stir in grated peel. Chill, stirring occasionally, until mixture is thick enough to coat the spoon, about 30 minutes.
- Meanwhile, in a medium bowl, beat egg whites until soft peaks form. Gradually beat in remaining 1/2 cup (125 mL) sugar until egg whites are stiff. Blend into cooled gelatin mixture.
- In a medium bowl, using an electric mixer or hand blender, beat whipping cream. In a small bowl, using the same beaters, purée tofu. Then beat tofu into whipped cream; fold into gelatin mixture. Pour filling into pie crust. Chill until set.
- To serve, garnish with lime slices and Best Whipped Topping, if desired.

makes 8 servings
preparation time: 40 minutes
chilling time: 4 hours to overnight

PER SERVING: 379 calories, 8 g protein, 47 g carbohydrate, 19 g total fat (8 g sat fat, 4 g mono fat, 1 g poly fat), 89 mg cholesterol, 2 g dietary fiber, 142 RE vitamin A, 8 mcg folate, 6 mg vitamin C, 33 mg calcium, 1 mg iron, 125 mg potassium, 86 mg sodium

quick lime cheesecake pie
1-bowl recipe

WE ALL need a few quick and easy recipes in our dessert repertoire. This is one of mine. It also happens to be one of my daughter Lara's favorite desserts.

	lime and kiwi topping (below)	
16 oz.	**soy cream cheese**	**500 g**
1¼ cups	**sweetened condensed milk**	**300 mL**
⅓ cup	**fresh lime juice, strained**	**75 mL**
2 tsp.	**grated lime peel**	**10 mL**
9-inch	**Graham Cracker Crust, page 63**	**23 cm**

- In a large bowl, with an electric mixer or hand blender, beat cream cheese with condensed milk until smooth. Gradually beat in lime juice and peel. Pour into pie crust. Cover and chill at least 4 hours.
- Just before serving, spoon Lime and Kiwi Topping over pie.

lime and kiwi topping

¼ cup	**fresh lime juice**	**60 mL**
½ cup	**water**	**125 mL**
¼ cup	**granulated sugar, or, to taste**	**60 mL**
2 tsp.	**cornstarch**	**10 mL**
2–3	**ripe kiwis, peeled, halved, and thinly sliced**	**2–3**

- In a small saucepan, combine juice, water, sugar, and cornstarch. Cook over medium heat, stirring constantly until mixture boils and thickens. Add kiwis, return to a boil, then remove from heat. Cover and chill at least 4 hours or overnight.

makes 8 servings
preparation time: filling, 10 minutes
topping, 10 minutes
chilling time: 4 hours to overnight

PER SERVING (WITH TOPPING): 599 calories, 12 g protein, 69 g carbohydrate, 32 g total fat (12 g sat fat, 3 g mono fat, 13 g poly fat), 38 mg cholesterol, 2 g dietary fiber, 131 RE vitamin A, 16 mcg folate, 26 mg vitamin C, 201 mg calcium, 1 mg iron, 355 mg potassium, 417 mg sodium

PER SERVING (WITHOUT TOPPING): 558 calories, 11 g protein, 58 g carbohydrate, 32 g total fat (12 g sat fat, 3 g mono fat, 13 g poly fat), 38 mg cholesterol, 2 g dietary fiber, 128 RE vitamin A, 9 mcg folate, 10 mg vitamin C, 195 mg calcium, < .5 mg iron, 284 mg potassium, 416 mg sodium

mango and lemon cheesecake pie

THIS IS absolutely divine: sweet mellow mango combined with tart lemon and soy cream cheese, topped with a thin layer of meringue. Make this your next dessert!

filling

8 oz.	soy cream cheese	250 g
1¼ cups	sweetened condensed milk	300 mL
2	egg yolks	2
½ cup	fresh lemon juice	125 mL
1	ripe mango, peeled and puréed	1
2 tbsp.	soy flour	30 mL
9-inch	Graham Cracker Crust, page 63	14 cm

meringue

2	egg whites	2
	pinch of cream of tartar	
1 tbsp.	granulated sugar	15 mL

- Preheat oven to 350° F (180° C).
- In a medium bowl, using an electric mixer or hand blender, blend together cream cheese, condensed milk, and egg yolks. Blend in lemon juice, puréed mango, and flour. Pour mixture into crust.
- Bake 35 to 40 minutes. Shortly before filling is baked, prepare meringue. In a small bowl, beat egg whites with cream of tartar until soft peaks form. Add sugar and beat until whites are stiff. Spread over hot pie filling. Broil until golden brown, 3 to 5 minutes. Cool completely.

makes 8–10 servings
preparation time: filling, 20 minutes
crust, 10 minutes
baking time: 35–40 minutes

PER SERVING: 299 calories, 5 g protein, 36 g carbohydrate, 15 g total fat (3 g sat fat, 3 g mono fat, 6 g poly fat), 43 mg cholesterol, 1 g dietary fiber, 151 RE vitamin A, 15 mcg folate, 12 mg calcium, 1 mg iron, 79 mg potassium, 274 mg sodium

sweet potato pie
non-dairy

THIS LIGHT version of a perennial Thanksgiving dessert tastes great after a rich turkey dinner.

1	single unbaked Sweet Pastry Crust, page 64	23 cm
2 cups	mashed sweet potatoes, canned or fresh	500 mL
¾ cup	granulated sugar	175 mL
¼ cup	brown sugar	60 mL
1 tbsp.	butter or margarine, melted	15 mL
2 tbsp.	fresh lemon juice	30 mL
½ tsp.	ground nutmeg	2 mL
1 tsp.	ground cinnamon	5 mL
1 tsp.	vanilla extract	5 mL
¼ tsp.	salt	1 mL
1 tsp.	grated lemon peel	5 mL
1	large egg	1
2	egg whites, beaten	2
⅔ cup	soft tofu, puréed	150 mL

- Press dough firmly against bottom and sides of ungreased pie plate.
- Preheat oven to 400° F (200° C).
- In a large bowl, using an electric mixer or hand blender, blend together all filling ingredients until smooth. Pour into prepared crust.
- Bake 20 minutes. Reduce oven temperature to 325° F (165° C) and bake another 20 minutes or until crust is golden and filling almost set. Cool on wire rack. Serve with Brown Sugar and Soynut Whipped Topping, below, if desired.

makes 8 servings
preparation time: crust, 15 minutes
filling, 20 minutes
baking time: 40 minutes

VARIATIONS: For the filling, use mashed pumpkin or squash. For a nutty flavored pie crust, use the Honey-Roasted Soynut Crust, page 78.

brown sugar and soynut whipped topping

½ cup	whipping cream	125 mL
⅓ cup	soft tofu	75 mL
2 tbsp.	packed brown sugar	30 mL
1 tbsp.	crushed honey-roasted soynuts	15 mL

- In a medium bowl, whip cream.
- In a separate bowl, using the same beaters, beat tofu with sugar until smooth. Blend into whipped cream. Fold in crushed soynuts.

makes about 1 cup
preparation time: 15 minutes
chilling time: 1 hour

PER SERVING: 358 calories, 7 g protein, 52 g carbohydrate, 15 g total fat (8 g sat fat, 4 g mono fat, 1 g poly fat), 85 mg cholesterol, 1 g dietary fiber, 145 RE vitamin A, 7 mcg folate, 2 vitamin C, 25 mg calcium, 2 mg iron, 92 mg potassium, 180 mg sodium

sugar pie

A CANADIAN favorite, sugar pie or "tarte au sucre" is especially popular in Quebec. I have reduced the sugar, cream, and butter called for in the original recipe but have kept enough of these key ingredients to maintain the sweet rich taste associated with this beloved pie.

2	single unbaked Pastry Crusts for Fruit Pies and Tarts, page 61	2
2¹⁄₂ cups	brown sugar	625 mL
3 tbsp.	unbleached flour	45 mL
1 tbsp.	soy flour	15 mL
1 cup + 1 tbsp.	vanilla soy milk	250 + 15 mL
¹⁄₂ cup	whipping cream	125 mL
1 tbsp.	butter	15 mL
2 tbsp.	light corn syrup	30 mL

- Make pastry; cover and chill until ready to use.
- To make the filling, whisk all ingredients together except for one tbsp. (15 mL) soy milk, in a medium saucepan. Over medium heat, bring mixture to a boil, whisking constantly to prevent lumping (or to smooth out any lumps that may have formed). When thickened, remove from heat, cover, and cool to room temperature.
- Preheat oven to 375° F (190° C).
- Roll out pastry into two 11-inch (28 cm) rounds. Line 9-inch (23 cm) pie plate with one and pour filling into it. Cut four to six slits into top pastry, then cover filling with it. Cut off excess dough, if any, and crimp edges. Brush crust with remaining 1 tbsp. (15 mL) soy milk.
- Bake 40 to 45 minutes or until crust is golden brown. Cool completely before serving.

makes 8 servings
preparation time: pastry, 20 minutes
filling, 15 minutes
baking time: 40–45 minutes
freezes well

PER SERVING: 504 calories, 11 g protein, 69 g carbohydrate, 22 g total fat (12 g sat fat, 6 g mono fat, 1 g poly fat), 109 mg cholesterol, 2 g dietary fiber, 208 RE vitamin A, 27 mcg folate, < .5 mg vitamin C, 59 mg calcium, 3 mg iron, 223 mg potassium, 90 mg sodium

butter tarts

THESE DELICIOUS tarts are loaded with nutritious ingredients including extra soy protein from the textured soy protein.

12	unbaked 3-inch tart shells or 24 mini tart shells	12 x 7.5 cm
½ cup	packed brown sugar	125 mL
½ cup	corn syrup	125 mL
1	egg	1
1 tbsp.	soybean oil	15 mL
¼ cup	soy milk	60 mL
1 tbsp.	TSP (textured soy protein), *or* 1 tsp. cornstarch	15 mL
¼ cup each	raisins and chopped pecans	60 mL

- Preheat oven to 375° F (190° C).
- In a medium bowl, whisk together brown sugar, corn syrup, egg, oil, and soy milk. Fold in TSP, raisins, and pecans. Spoon filling into tart shells to ¾ full. Bake about 15 minutes or until filling is bubbly and pastry is golden. Cool on wire rack.

makes 12 3-inch (7.5 cm) or 24 mini tart shells.
preparation time: 15 minutes
baking time: 15 minutes
freezes well

PER MINI TART: 128 calories, 1 g protein, 18 g carbohydrate, 6 g total fat (2 g sat fat, 2 g mono fat, 1 g poly fat), 12 mg cholesterol, < .5 g dietary fiber*, 4 RE vitamin A*, 1 mcg folate*, < .5 mg vitamin C*, 7 mg calcium*, < .5 mg iron*, 42 mg potassium*, 13 mg sodium*

PER 3-INCH (7.5 cm) TART: 217 calories, 2 g protein, 32 g carbohydrate, 10 g total fat (3 g sat fat, 3 g mono fat, 1 g poly fat), 22 mg cholesterol, < .5 g dietary fiber*, 7 RE vitamin A*, 3 mcg folate*, < .5 mg vitamin C*, 14 mg calcium*, < .5 mg iron*, 84 mg potassium*, 26 mg sodium*

creamy rhubarb tart
non-dairy

THE NUTTY-flavored crust, which nicely complements the tangy cream filling, makes this a treat you'll want to enjoy year round. Although rhubarb season begins in late April and lasts most of the summer, diced rhubarb freezes well. By stashing some in your freezer, you can make this delicious tart even during the off-season.

9-inch	unbaked Honey-Roasted Soynut Crust, page 78	23 cm
4 cups	cubed fresh or frozen rhubarb, thawed	I L
8 oz.	(container) soy sour cream	250 mL
2 tsp.	vanilla extract	10 mL
1 cup	granulated sugar	250 mL
¼ cup	soy flour	60 mL
1 tsp.	grated lemon peel	5 mL

crunchy topping

2 tbsp.	brown sugar	30 mL
1 tbsp.	soy flour	15 mL
1 tbsp.	crushed roasted soynuts	15 mL
1–2 tbsp.	butter	15–30 mL

- Roll out pastry to fit bottom and sides of a 9- or 10-inch (23 or 25 cm) ungreased tart pan with a removable bottom.
- Preheat oven to 350° F (180° C).
- Place cubed rhubarb in a large bowl.
- In a separate bowl, whisk together sour cream, vanilla, sugar, flour, and lemon peel until smooth. Pour mixture over rhubarb and stir to coat fruit. Transfer filling to pie shell.
- *To make the topping*, combine sugar, flour, and soynuts. Sprinkle over rhubarb. Dot with butter.
- Bake 30 to 40 minutes, or until fruit is tender and crust is golden. Cool completely on wire rack.

makes 8 servings
preparation time: crust, 10 minutes
filling and topping, 10 minutes

PER SERVING: 357 calories, 11 g protein, 46 g carbohydrate, 16 g total fat (8 g sat fat, 3 g mono fat, 3 g poly fat), 25 mg cholesterol, 5 g dietary fiber, 101 RE vitamin A, 5 mcg folate, 5 mg vitamin C, 73 mg calcium, 2 mg iron, 189 mg potassium, 197 mg sodium

lemon-lime tart

non-dairy

I LOVE everything lemony, so this refreshingly tangy custard in a light buttery soy crust is a temptation I can't resist.

9-inch	single, unbaked Pastry Crust for Fruit Pies, and Tarts page 61	23 cm
¼ cup	fresh lemon juice	60 mL
¼ cup	fresh lime juice	60 mL
2	eggs	2
1	egg white	1
½ cup	granulated sugar	125 mL
2 tbsp.	soy milk	30 mL
1 tbsp.	butter or margarine, melted	15 mL

- Roll out pastry to fit bottom and sides of a 9-inch (23 cm) tart pan with removable bottom.
- Preheat oven to 400° F (200° C). In a medium bowl, using an electric mixer or hand blender, blend juice, eggs, egg white, sugar, soy milk, and butter until smooth. Pour mixture into pie crust.
- Bake 35 to 40 minutes, or until crust is golden and filling just set. Remove from oven and cool to room temperature.

makes 8 servings
preparation time: crust, 15 minutes
filling, 15 minutes
baking time: 35–40 minutes
freezes well

PER SERVING: 201 calories, 7 g protein, 23 g carbohydrate, 10 g total fat (5 g sat fat, 3 g mono fat, 1 g poly fat), 93 mg cholesterol, 1 g dietary fiber, 100 RE vitamin A, 10 mcg folate, 6 mg vitamin C, 12 mg calcium, 1 mg iron, 47 mg potassium, 50 mg sodium

mango kiwi soynut tart

THIS NUTTY soy crust contrasts wonderfully with the silky smoothness of the creamy soy filling. Topped with fresh mango, kiwi, and raspberry glaze, this makes a gorgeous finale to a celebratory meal.

honey-roasted soynut crust

¾ cup	unbleached flour	175 mL
¼ cup	soy flour	60 mL
	pinch of salt	
¼ cup	crushed honey roasted soynuts	60 mL
⅓ cup	cold butter, cut up	75 mL
4–5 tbsp.	ice water	60–75 mL

filling

4 oz.	soy cream cheese	125 g
¼ cup	confectioner's sugar	60 mL
¼ cup	soft tofu	60 mL
⅓ cup	whipping cream, whipped	75 mL
1	egg white, beaten	1
1–2 tsp.	grated lemon peel	5–10 mL

fruit topping

2	ripe kiwis, peeled and cut into thin rounds	2
1	ripe mango, peeled and cut into small cubes	1
3 tbsp.	raspberry jelly	45 mL

- Preheat oven to 375° F (190° C).

- *To make the crust,* stir together flours, salt, and soynuts. With a pastry blender, cut in butter until mixture resembles coarse crumbs. Gradually stir in enough water to shape dough into a ball. Cover and chill (or freeze) until ready to use.

- On a lightly floured surface, roll dough to fit bottom and sides of a 10-inch (25 cm) tart pan with a removable bottom. Fold dough in half (to prevent tearing) and transfer to pan, pressing it against the fluted sides.

- Line pastry shell with foil. Bake 10 minutes. Remove foil. Bake another 10 minutes, or until golden. Cool on wire rack.

- *To make the filling,* place the cream cheese, confectioner's sugar, and tofu in a medium bowl. Using an electric mixer or hand blender, beat until smooth. Fold in whipped cream, beaten egg white, and grated lemon peel. Spread evenly over cooled tart shell.

- *To make the fruit topping,* arrange kiwi slices in an overlapping pattern around the outer crust. Place mango cubes in the center.

- Heat jelly and drizzle over fruit. Chill 1 hour. Gently remove sides of tart pan and transfer tart to a serving platter.

makes 8 or 9 servings
preparation time: crust, 10 minutes
filling, 15 minutes
fruit topping, 10 minutes
baking time: 20 minutes

PER SERVING (PIE CRUST ONLY): 154 calories, 7 g protein, 13 g carbohydrate, 9 g total fat (5 g sat fat, 2 g mono fat, < .5 g poly fat), 21 mg cholesterol, 3 g dietary fiber, 71 RE vitamin A, < .5 mcg folate, 14 mg calcium, 1 mg iron, 2 mg potassium, 56 mg sodium

PER SERVING (TART): 256 calories, 8 g protein, 24 g carbohydrate, 15 g total fat (7 g sat fat, 3 g mono fat, 3 g poly fat), 30 mg cholesterol, 4 g dietary fiber, 198 RE vitamin A, 10 mcg folate, 23 mg vitamin C, 28 mg calcium, 1 mg iron, 120 mg potassium, 121 mg sodium

blueberry cheesecake tarts

WHEN YOU'VE invited a large crowd for a barbecue or party, these mini tarts are the perfect finger food dessert.

	Amaretto Cheesecake Filling, below	
24	commercial baked 3-inch tart shells, or 48 mini tart shells	24 x 7.5 cm
1 cup	blueberries	250 mL

- Make Amaretto Cheesecake Filling. Chill until ready to use.
- To assemble tarts, spoon filling into tart shells. Top with blueberries. Chill until ready to serve.

amaretto cheesecake filling

4 oz.	soy cream cheese	125 g
½ cup	soft tofu	125 mL
¼ cup	confectioner's sugar	60 mL
4 tsp.	Amaretto liqueur	20 mL
2 tsp.	ground almonds	10 mL
½ cup	whipping cream, whipped	125 mL

- In a medium bowl, cream together cream cheese, tofu, and confectioner's sugar. When smooth, mix in Amaretto and almonds. Fold in whipped cream. Chill until ready to fill tart shells.

makes 24 3-inch (7.5 cm) or 48 mini tart shells
preparation: 20 minutes

VARIATIONS: For a colorful presentation, use half blueberries, half raspberries, or any other seasonal fruit. Phyllo cups can be used instead of regular pastry shells.

PER MINI TART: 93 calories, 1 g protein, 8 g carbohydrate, 6 g total fat (2 g sat fat, 2 g mono fat, 1 g poly fat), 7 mg cholesterol, < .5 dietary fiber*, 12 RE vitamin A*, < .5 mcg folate*, < .5 mg vitamin C*, 3 mg calcium*, < .5 mg iron*, 8 mg potassium*, 13 mg sodium*

PER 3-INCH (7.5 cm) TART: 146 calories, 2 g protein, 12 g carbohydrate, 10 g total fat (4 g sat fat, 3 g mono fat, 2 g poly fat), 13 mg cholesterol, < .5 g dietary fiber*, 23 RE vitamin A*, < .5 mcg folate*, < .5 mg vitamin C*, 5 mg calcium*, < .5 mg iron*, 16 mg potassium*, 25 mg sodium*

orange mocha cheesecake tarts

NEED AN elegant dessert tonight? These dainty tarts take only minutes to prepare.

	Orange Mocha Cheesecake Cream, below	
24	commercial baked 3-inch tart shells, or 48 baked mini tart shells	24 x 7.5 cm
¼ cup	chocolate shavings (optional)	60 mL

- Make Orange Mocha Cheesecake Cream. Chill until ready to use.
- To assemble tarts, spoon cream into tart shells. Garnish with chocolate shavings, if desired.

orange mocha cheesecake cream

4 oz.	soy cream cheese	125 g
½ cup	soft tofu	125 mL
¼ cup	confectioner's sugar	60 mL
2 tsp.	unsweetened cocoa powder	10 mL
2–3 tsp.	grated orange peel	10–15 mL
1 tsp.	instant coffee granules	5 mL
1 tbsp.	water	15 mL
½ cup	whipping cream, whipped	125 mL

- In a medium bowl, cream together cream cheese, tofu, sugar, cocoa, and orange peel. Combine coffee and water and stir into cheese mixture. Fold in whipped cream. Chill until ready to fill tart shells.

makes 24 3-inch or 48 mini tart shells
preparation time: 20 minutes

PER MINI TART: 90 calories, 1 g protein, 8 g carbohydrate, 6 g total fat (2 g sat fat, 2 g mono fat, 1 g poly fat), 7 mg cholesterol, < .5 g dietary fiber*, 12 RE vitamin A*, < .5 mcg folate*, < .5 mg vitamin C*, 3 mg calcium*, < .5 mg iron*, 9 mg potassium*, 12 mg sodium*

PER 3-INCH (7.5cm) TART: 139 calories, 2 g protein, 11 g carbohydrate, 10 g total fat (4 g sat fat, 3 g mono fat, 2 g poly fat), 13 mg cholesterol, < .5 g dietary fiber*, 23 RE vitamin A*, < .5 mcg folate*, < .5 mg vitamin C*, 6 mg calcium*, < .5 mg iron*, 18 mg potassium*, 25 mg sodium*

chocolate orange pear tart
non-dairy

A SPECIAL dessert for a special occasion. Can be made one day ahead.

9-inch	Flan Pastry Crust, page 62	23 cm
2 oz.	semi-sweet chocolate, shaved or grated, divided	56 g
3–4	medium ripe pears	3–4
1	egg	1
¾ cup	vanilla soy milk	175 mL
2 tbsp.	fresh orange juice	30 mL
2 tsp.	grated orange rind	10 mL
2 tbsp.	Grand Marnier or orange brandy	30 mL
1 tbsp.	soy flour	15 mL
1 tbsp.	coarsely chopped soynuts (optional)	15 mL
1 tbsp.	brown sugar	15 mL

- Prepare pie crust and press onto bottom and side of a 9- or 10-inch (23 or 25 cm) tart pan. Spread shaved chocolate, except for 2 tbsp. (30 mL), over pastry.
- Preheat oven to 375° F (190° C).
- Peel, halve, and thinly slice pears. Arrange overlapping slices in pie shell.
- In a medium bowl, with electric mixer or hand blender, beat together egg, soy milk, orange juice, rind, Grand Marnier, and flour until smooth. Pour evenly over pears. Sprinkle with soynuts, if using, and brown sugar.
- Bake 50 to 60 minutes, or until puffy and golden. Cool to room temperature. Garnish with remaining 2 tbsp. (30 mL) chocolate shavings.

makes 8 servings
preparation time: pastry, 15 minutes
filling, 20 minutes
baking time: 50–60 minutes
freezes well

PER SERVING: 287 calories, 6 g protein, 31 g carbohydrate, 15 g total fat (8 g sat fat, 4 g mono fat, 1 g poly fat), 78 mg cholesterol, 2 g dietary fiber, 131 RE vitamin A, 12 mcg folate, 5 mg vitamin C, 19 mg calcium, 2 mg iron, 141 mg potassium, 70 mg sodium

summer berry pizza

ENJOY THIS refreshing tart when berries are ripe and bursting with flavor. Any combination of berries will do.

	Lemon Curd, page 174	
1	Honey-Roasted Soynut Crust, page 78	1
5–6 cups	fresh mixed berries	1.25–1.50 L
4–6 tbsp.	black currant jelly	60–90 mL

- Make lemon curd. Cover and chill until ready to use.
- Make crust and roll out to fit a 12-inch (30 cm) pizza pan. Bake according to crust recipe directions. Let cool on wire rack.
- Spread chilled lemon curd over cooled pastry.
- Arrange berries attractively in a circular pattern on lemon curd.
- Heat jelly and drizzle over berries. Serve with Best Whipped Topping, page 170, if desired.

makes 8 or 9 servings
preparation time: lemon curd, 15 minutes*
crust, 10 minutes
baking time: 20 minutes
freezes well

*Reduce preparation time by making the lemon curd 1 day ahead.

PER SERVING: 231 calories, 6 g protein, 37 g carbohydrate, 8 g total fat (4 g sat fat, 2 g mono fat, < .5 g poly fat), 79 mg cholesterol, 2 g dietary fiber, 77 RE vitamin A, 10 mcg folate, 23 mg vitamin C, 11 mg calcium, 1 mg iron, 44 mg potassium, 41 mg sodium

apple turnovers
non-dairy

ON A cold winter day, is there anything more inviting than the aroma of apple turnovers baking in the oven? The pastry is also suitable for pies.

pastry

2 cups	unbleached flour	500 mL
¼ cup	soy flour	60 mL
1 tsp.	sugar	5 mL
½ tsp.	salt	2 mL
½ cup	chilled butter or margarine	125 mL
½ cup	chilled vanilla soy milk	125 mL
¼–½ cup	ice water	60–125 mL

filling

2 tbsp.	soy flour	30 mL
½ cup	sugar (more if apples are tart)	125 mL
5–6	medium apples, peeled, cored and halved	5–6
	ground cinnamon, to taste	
3 tbsp.	vanilla soy milk	45 mL
	sugar, for sprinkling	

- In a large bowl, combine flours, sugar, and salt. Mix in butter with a pastry blender until mixture resembles coarse crumbs. Add soy milk and ¼ cup (60 mL) water. Mix until the dough just comes together. If mixture is too dry, add remaining water. Shape dough into a ball. Flatten ball and divide dough into 10 to 12 equal parts (depending on the size of the apples). On a floured surface, roll each into a thin 8 x 5-inch (20 x 13 cm) oval.

- Spoon about 1 tsp. (5 mL) each, flour and sugar, on one half of each oval. Place half an apple, cut side down, on top. Sprinkle with cinnamon and a little more sugar. Fold the long half of the oval over the apple, then fold the edge of the bottom half up over the edge of the top half; press to seal and flute the edge. Brush the top of the turnovers with soy milk and sprinkle with sugar.

- Bake on ungreased nonstick cookie sheet in a 350° F (180° C) oven for 40 to 45 minutes until golden brown. Serve warm or at room temperature à la mode.

**makes 10–12 apple turnovers
preparation time: 60 minutes***
**baking time: 40–45 minutes
freezes well**

*Reduce preparation time by making the pastry ahead and freezing it.

PER TURNOVER: 217 calories, 4 g protein, 33 g carbohydrate, 8 g total fat (5 g sat fat, 2 g mono fat, < .5 g poly fat), 21 mg cholesterol, 2 g dietary fiber, 75 RE vitamin A, 2 mcg folate, 3 mg vitamin C, 7 mg calcium, 2 mg iron, 89 mg potassium, 101 mg sodium

pancakes, crepes, cobblers & dumplings

blueberry pancakes
non-dairy

I LOVE making these pancakes on a weekend morning when no one is rushed and we can enjoy a leisurely breakfast.

1 cup	unbleached flour	250 mL
1 cup	oat flour	250 mL
½ cup	soy flour	125 mL
1 tbsp.	baking powder	15 mL
½ tsp.	salt	2 mL
½ cup	brown sugar	125 mL
2	eggs	2
2–2½ cups	soy milk	500–625 mL
1 tsp.	grated lemon peel	5 mL
1 tbsp.	soybean oil	15 mL
2 cups	fresh or frozen* blueberries	500 mL

- In a large bowl, combine flours, baking powder, salt, and sugar.
- In a separate bowl, whisk together eggs, soy milk, lemon peel, and oil. Blend into flour mixture just until evenly moistened. Fold in berries.
- Heat a lightly greased nonstick frying pan. When pan is hot, pour in a ¼-cup (50 mL) ladle of batter. Cook over medium heat about 2 minutes, or until top of pancake is bubbly. Turn and cook another 2 minutes, or until pancake is well puffed. Keep warm while remaining pancakes are being cooked. To serve, top with syrup.

makes 20 medium pancakes
preparation time: 15 minutes
cooking time: 4 minutes per panful
freezes well

*If using frozen berries, blend them into batter while still frozen. This will prevent them from coloring the batter purple.

PER PANCAKE: 99 calories, 4 g protein, 17 g carbohydrate, 2 g total fat (< .5 g sat fat, < .5 g mono fat, 1 g poly fat), 19 mg cholesterol, 2 g dietary fiber, 12 RE vitamin A, 4 mcg folate, 4 mg vitamin C, 8 mg calcium, 1 mg iron, 78 mg potassium, 91 mg sodium

THESE SCRUMPTIOUS pancakes are a terrific way to use up any leftover bread.

4–5	slices white bread, cubed	4–5
2 cups	vanilla soy milk	500 mL
2	eggs, beaten	2
$1/4$ cup	soy flour	60 mL
1 tbsp.	sugar	15 mL
1 tsp.	ground cinnamon	5 mL
2	medium apples, peeled, cored, and grated	2
	sugar, for sprinkling, optional	

- Place bread cubes in a medium bowl. Pour soy milk over them and let stand a few minutes until milk is absorbed and bread is soft. Mash with a fork and blend in remaining ingredients. If the mixture is runny, add a little more flour.
- Heat a large, lightly greased nonstick frying pan over medium heat. Drop 2 heaping tbsp. (30 mL) of batter per pancake into the hot pan, spreading the mixture with the back of a fork so that it is about $1/2$-inch (1 cm) thick. Cook in batches of 3 or 4, about 3 minutes per side or until lightly browned. Sprinkle with sugar or serve with maple syrup.

makes approx. 16–20 pancakes
preparation time: 20 minutes
cooking time: 6 minutes per batch
freezes well

PER PANCAKE: 44 calories, 2 g protein, 7 g carbohydrate, 1 g total fat (< .5 g sat fat, < .5 g mono fat, < .5 poly fat), 19 mg cholesterol, 1 g dietary fiber, 10 RE vitamin A, 5 mcg folate, 1 mg vitamin C, 21 mg calcium, 1 mg iron, 57 mg potassium, 39 mg sodium

chocolate crêpes

non-dairy, 1-bowl recipe

ROLLED UP with maple syrup or your favorite cream or fruit filling, these crêpes are a delectable treat.

2 tbsp.	unsweetened cocoa powder	30 mL
4 oz.	soy cream cheese	125 g
½ cup	soft tofu	125 mL
2	eggs	2
1½ cups	soy milk	375 mL
1 cup	water	250 mL
1¼ cups	unbleached flour	310 mL
2 tbsp.	granulated sugar	30 mL
	pinch of salt	

- Sift cocoa into a large bowl. Using an electric mixer or hand blender, beat in cream cheese, tofu, and eggs. Blend in soy milk and water. Gradually beat in remaining ingredients until batter is smooth.
- Heat a lightly greased 8-inch (20 cm) nonstick frying pan or crêpe pan. When hot, pour enough batter to thinly coat bottom of pan. Quickly swirl to spread the batter evenly. Cook over medium heat 40 to 60 seconds until underside is lightly browned. Loosen edge with a spatula and turn out onto plate. Stack crêpes to prevent them from drying out. Serve immediately or cover and chill until ready to use, up to 2 days. Reheat in microwave oven before serving.

makes about 20 8-inch (20 cm) crêpes
preparation time: 10 minutes
cooking time: 1 minute per panful
freezes well

PER CRÊPE: 64 calories, 2 g protein, 8 g carbohydrate, 3 g total fat (1 g sat fat, < .5 g mono fat, 1 g poly fat), 19 mg cholesterol, 1 g dietary fiber, 12 RE vitamin A, 2 mcg folate, < .5 mg vitamin C, 6 mg calcium, 1 mg iron, 69 mg potassium, 35 mg sodium

french toast with fried apples

A CLASSIC brunch offering French toast can also be served for lunch or as a healthy snack, especially when complemented with fruit.

fried apples

1 tbsp.	butter or margarine	15 mL
2	medium apples, peeled, cored, halved, and sliced	2
2 tbsp.	granulated sugar (or to taste)	30 mL
2 tbsp.	soy milk	30 mL
	ground cinnamon, to taste	

- In a medium nonstick frying pan, over high heat, melt butter. Add apples and sugar. Fry until evenly browned. Stir in soy milk and sprinkle with cinnamon. Reduce heat and simmer, stirring occasionally, 5 to 10 minutes. Keep warm until ready to serve.

french toast

4	eggs	4
½ cup	soft tofu	125 mL
¾ cup	vanilla soy milk	175 mL
	pinch of salt	
8–10	slices of bread (depending on thickness)	8–10

- In a medium bowl, with an electric hand blender, blend together eggs, tofu, soy milk, and salt. Dip bread slices into egg mixture and let soak 1 to 2 minutes, or until soaked through.
- In a large, lightly greased, nonstick frying pan, fry bread slices over medium heat for 2 minutes per side, or until golden brown.
- Serve warm, topped with fried apples. If you want to splurge, drizzle with Caramel Sauce, page 172.

makes 4–5 servings
preparation time: fried apples, 10 minutes
                French toast, 10 minutes
cooking time: fried apples, 10 minutes
                French toast per panful, 4 minutes

PER SERVING: 266 calories, 10 g protein, 38 g carbohydrate, 9 g total fat (3 g sat fat, 2 g mono fat, 1 g poly fat), 156 mg cholesterol, 2 g dietary fiber, 95 RE vitamin A, 19 mcg folate, 5 mg vitamin C, 160 mg calcium, 3 mg iron, 217 mg potassium, 292 mg sodium

peach fritters
non-dairy

FRITTERS ARE always a hit, especially these tasty ones made with fresh ripe peaches.

	Fruit Fritter Batter, page 140	
4	medium ripe peaches, peeled and chopped	4
	oil for deep-frying	
	granulated sugar for sprinkling (optional)	

- Make fritter batter. Fold chopped peaches into batter.
- In a wok or deep frying pan, heat enough oil to cover fritters (about 3 in./7 ½ cm. deep). Heat oil to 365° F (185° C) or until bubbles start to form. Make the fritters in several batches. Scoop up a heaping tablespoon of batter and, with another spoon, scrape it into the hot oil. Work close to the oil to prevent splattering.
- Fry fritters 3 to 5 minutes, turning them for even browning. Remove fritters with a slotted spoon and drain on paper towels. Sprinkle with sugar and transfer to a serving platter. Serve as soon as possible.

makes about 20 fritters
preparation time: 20 minutes
cooking time: 15 minutes

VARIATIONS: Instead of peaches, try chopped apples or sliced bananas.

PER FRITTER: 45 calories, 2 g protein, 9 g carbohydrate, < .5 g total fat (< .5 g sat fat, < .5 g mono fat, < .5 g poly fat), 9 mg cholesterol, 1 g dietary fiber, 15 RE vitamin A, 2 mcg folate, 1 mg vitamin C, 2 mg calcium, < .5 mg iron, 53 mg potassium, 33 mg sodium

USE THIS versatile batter for any chopped fruits or berries.

1 cup	unbleached flour	250 mL
⅓ cup	soy flour	75 mL
	pinch of salt	
2 tsp.	baking powder	10 mL
2 tbsp.	sugar	30 mL
1	egg, beaten	1
⅔ cup	vanilla-flavored soy milk	150 mL

- In a medium bowl, combine dry ingredients. Mix in egg and soy milk to make a smooth batter. If batter is too thick to stir in fruit, add a little more soy milk. Pan-fry or deep-fry fritters according to recipe directions.

PER FRITTER: 37 calories, 2 g protein, 7 g carbohydrate, < .5 g total fat (< .5 g sat fat, < .5 mono fat, < .5 g poly fat), 9 mg cholesterol, < .5 g dietary fiber, 4 RE vitamin A, 1 mcg folate, 1 mg calcium, < .5 mg iron, 14 mg potassium, 33 mg sodium

maple grandpères

THESE DOUGHY dumplings simmered in sweet maple syrup are a specialty of Quebec, where maple syrup is plentiful. I've added protein-rich soy flour and soy milk to the traditional recipe and reduced the butter and syrup. Serve them for breakfast or brunch.

1 1/2 cups	maple syrup	375 mL
1 cup	water	250 mL
1 1/4 cups	unbleached flour	310 mL
1/4 cup	soy flour	60 mL
1 tbsp.	baking powder	15 mL
1/4 tsp.	salt	1 mL
3 tbsp.	butter or margarine	45 mL
3/4 cup	soy milk	175 mL

- In a large saucepan, combine maple syrup and water; bring to a boil.
- In a medium bowl, combine dry ingredients. Cut in butter with a pastry blender until mixture resembles coarse crumbs. Stir in enough soy milk to make a soft dough.
- Drop dough by small spoonfuls into the boiling mixture. Cover and reduce heat to low; simmer 12 to 15 minutes without lifting the lid. Serve warm.

makes 15 to 18 dumplings
preparation time: 10 minutes
cooking time: 12 to 15 minutes

PER DUMPLING: 121 calories, 2 g protein, 24 g carbohydrate, 2 g total fat (1 g sat fat, 1 g mono fat, < .5 g poly fat), 5 mg cholesterol, < .5 g dietary fiber, 18 RE vitamin A, < .5 mcg folate, 19 mg calcium, 1 mg iron, 69 mg potassium, 103 mg sodium

honey rum baked apples
non-dairy

THIS RECIPE is easy to multiply to suit your needs. A little extra protein in the form of textured soy protein (TSP) acts as a thickening agent here.

1	apple	1
2 tsp.	honey-roasted soynuts	10 mL
2 tsp.	TSP (textured soy protein)	10 mL
1 tbsp.	liquid honey	15 mL
2 tbsp.	soy milk	30 mL
1 tbsp.	rum	15 mL
	ground cinnamon, to taste	

- Preheat oven to 375° F (190° C).
- Slice apple in half. Core to form 2 small cavities. Place apple halves, cut side up, in a small baking dish. Fill cavities with soynuts and TSP.
- Combine honey, soy milk, and rum; spoon half the mixture over the apples and filling. Sprinkle with cinnamon.
- Bake about 20 minutes. Spoon remaining honey mixture over apples. Bake 20 to 25 minutes longer, or until apples are tender. To serve, place on dessert plates and top with syrup from pan.

makes 2 servings
preparation time: 10 minutes
baking time: 40–45 minutes

VARIATION: To reduce baking time, cook apple halves in microwave oven, on high, for 2–3 minutes, then in regular oven for 20–30 minutes.

PER SERVING: 130 calories, 4 g protein, 23 g carbohydrate, 2 g total fat ($<$ .5 g sat fat, $<$ .5 g mono fat, $<$ .5 g poly fat), 4 g dietary fiber, 4 RE vitamin A, 6 mcg folate, 4 mg vitamin C, 19 mg calcium, 1 mg iron, 136 mg potassium, 47 mg sodium

pear and cherry crisp with lemon sauce
non-dairy

A PLEASANT change from the usual apple crisp, this is no ordinary dessert. The creamy tangy lemon sauce complements the natural sweetness of the pears and dried cherries.

5	medium ripe pears, peeled and thinly sliced	5
¼–½ cup	dried Bing Cherries	60–125 mL
6 oz.	(container) vanilla soy yogurt	175 g
1 tbsp.	granulated sugar	15 mL
1 tsp.	grated lemon peel	5 mL
1 tsp.	fresh lemon juice	5 mL
1 tsp.	soy flour (if pears are very juicy)	5 mL
¼ cup	packed brown sugar	60 mL
2 tbsp. each	rolled oats, wheat germ, and soy flakes	30 mL
	Lemon Sauce, below	

- Preheat oven to 375° F (190° C).
- In a medium bowl, combine sliced pears and cherries.
- In a separate bowl, whisk together yogurt, sugar, lemon peel, lemon juice, and soy flour, if needed. Fold into pears and cherries. Transfer to a 9-inch (23 cm) square baking dish.
- In a small bowl, combine brown sugar, oats, wheat germ, and soy flakes. Spoon over fruit.
- Bake 30 to 40 minutes, or until pears are tender. Serve warm or at room temperature with a dollop of lemon sauce on the side.

makes 4–6 servings
preparation time: 15 minutes
baking time: 30–40 minutes

⅓ cup	granulated sugar	75 mL
2 tsp.	cornstarch	10 mL
1 cup	soy milk	250 mL
1	egg yolk	1
½ tsp.	grated lemon peel	2 mL
2–3 tbsp.	fresh lemon juice	30–45 mL

- In a medium saucepan, combine sugar and cornstarch. Stir in 2 tbsp. of the soy milk until smooth. Gradually whisk in rest of soy milk. Cook and continue to whisk over medium heat until thickened and bubbly. Remove from heat.
- In a small bowl, stir a spoonful of the hot mixture into the egg yolk. Pour back into saucepan; cook and stir over low heat until nearly bubbly. Stir in lemon peel and juice. Remove from heat. Serve warm or cover and chill until ready to serve.

makes about 2 cups (500 ml)
preparation time: 10 minutes

PER SERVING: 206 calories, 5 g protein, 44 g carbohydrate, 3 g total fat (< .5 g sat fat, < .5 g mono fat, < .5 g poly fat), 5 g dietary fiber, 8 RE vitamin A, 20 mcg folate, 8 mg vitamin C, 32 mg calcium, 1 mg iron, 283 mg potassium, 12 mg sodium

PER TBSP (LEMON SAUCE): 13 calories, < .5 g protein, 2 g carbohydrate, < .5 g total fat (< .5 g sat fat, < .5 g mono fat, < .5 g poly fat), 6 mg cholesterol, < .5 g dietary fiber, 3 RE vitamin A, 1 mcg folate, < .5 mg vitamin C, 1 mg calcium, < .5 mg iron, 12 mg potassium, 1 mg sodium

pancakes, crepes, cobblers & dumplings

black forest cobbler

COBBLERS ARE the perfect comfort food on a chilly autumn or winter day. This one can be made ahead and reheated in the microwave oven just before serving.

6 cups	frozen pitted sour cherries, with juice	1.5 L
½ cup	sugar	125 mL
2 tbsp.	cornstarch	30 mL
1 tbsp.	brandy	15 mL
¾ cup	unbleached flour	175 mL
2 tbsp.	soy flour	30 mL
3 tbsp.	unsweetened cocoa powder	45 mL
2 tbsp.	granulated sugar	30 mL
1½ tsp.	baking powder	7 mL
	pinch of salt	
2 tbsp.	butter or margarine	30 mL
1 cup	soy milk	250 mL

- In a medium saucepan, combine cherries, ½ cup (125 mL) sugar, and cornstarch. Bring to a boil, stirring constantly, until mixture thickens. Stir in brandy. Pour into an ungreased 8-inch (20 cm) square baking dish.
- Preheat oven to 400° F (200° C). Place cherries in oven to keep hot.
- In medium bowl, combine flours, cocoa, 2 tbsp. (30 mL) sugar, baking powder, and salt. Mix in butter with a pastry blender until mixture is evenly crumbly. Stir in soy milk to form a smooth firm batter. Drop 6 spoonfuls of batter onto hot cherry mixture.
- Bake 25 minutes, or until toothpick inserted in biscuit comes out clean. Serve warm with ice cream, if desired.

makes 6 servings
preparation time: 15 minutes
baking time: 25 minutes

PER SERVING: 288 calories, 6 g protein, 55 g carbohydrate, 6 g total fat (3 g sat fat, < .5 mono fat, 1 g poly fat), 12 mg cholesterol, 4 g dietary fiber, 136 RE vitamin A, 32 mcg folate, 3 mg vitamin C, 28 mg calcium, 3 mg iron, 394 mg potassium, 82 mg sodium

nutty cranberry cobbler

A FAST and easy treat that is delicious and healthy; you can make this cobbler all year round with different berries and fruits.

3 cups	cranberries, fresh or frozen	750 mL
½ cup	chopped macadamia nuts	125 mL
2 tbsp.	toasted soy flakes	30 mL
1½ cups	granulated sugar, divided	375 mL
1	egg	1
1	egg white	1
¼ cup	soft tofu	60 mL
¼ cup	butter, melted	60 mL
¼ cup	soybean oil	60 mL
2 tbsp.	orange juice	30 mL
1 tbsp.	grated orange peel	15 mL
³/₄ cup	unbleached flour	175 mL
¼ cup	soy flour	60 mL
½ tsp.	baking powder	2 mL

- Preheat oven to 325° F (165° C). Grease and flour a deep 10-inch (25 cm) pie plate.
- Spread cranberries in pie plate. Sprinkle with nuts, soy flakes, and ½ cup (125 mL) sugar.
- In a medium bowl, using an electric mixer or hand blender, blend together remaining 1 cup (250 mL) sugar, egg, egg white, tofu, butter, oil, orange juice, and peel. Mix in flours and baking powder to form a smooth thick batter. Spoon over cranberries.
- Bake 35 to 45 minutes, or until fruit is bubbly and top is golden. Cut into wedges and serve warm or at room temperature. Great with Best Whipped Topping (page 170) or ice cream.

makes about 10 servings
preparation time: 15 minutes
baking time: 35–45 minutes

VARIATIONS: Instead of cranberries, try blueberries or sliced peaches or apricots. The sugar content may need to be adjusted.

PER SERVING: 334 calories, 6 g protein, 44 g carbohydrate, 17 g total fat (5 g sat fat, 5 g mono fat, < .5 g poly fat), 31 mg cholesterol, 3 g dietary fiber, 54 RE vitamin A, 4 mcg folate, 6 mg vitamin C, 14 mg calcium, 1 mg iron, 76 mg potassium, 29 mg sodium

pancakes, crepes, cobblers & dumplings

strawberry shortcake
non-dairy

WHOLESOME, LIGHT and low-fat cream cheese biscuits make a perfect base for this classically delicious strawberry shortcake.

cream cheese biscuits

2½ cups	unbleached flour	625 mL
2 tbsp.	rolled oats	30 mL
2 tbsp.	granulated sugar	30 mL
½ tsp.	salt	2 mL
3 tsp.	baking powder	45 mL
2 tbsp.	butter or margarine	30 mL
2 tbsp.	soy cream cheese	30 mL
½ cup	soft tofu, puréed	125 mL
½ cup	soy milk	125 mL
2 cups	Best Whipped Topping, page 170	500 mL

sweetened strawberries

6 cups	fresh strawberries	1.5 kg
½ cup	granulated sugar	125 mL

- Preheat oven to 400° F (200° C).
- *To make sweetened strawberries,* crush ¼ of the berries and slice the remainder, place them in a bowl, sprinkle with sugar and allow to marinate a few hours in the refrigerator before serving.
- *To make the biscuits,* in a medium bowl, combine flour, oats, sugar, salt, and baking powder. Mix in butter and cream cheese with a pastry blender until mixture is evenly crumbled. Work in tofu and soy milk and knead a few seconds until dough holds together. Roll or pat to ¾-inch (2 cm) thickness. Cut into 2-inch (5 cm) rounds with a cookie cutter and place rounds on an ungreased cookie sheet about 1 inch (2.5 cm) apart.
- Bake about 18 minutes. Meanwhile, make Best Whipped Topping.
- *To make Strawberry Shortcake,* cut hot biscuits in half horizontally. Fill and top with sweetened strawberries. Top with Best Whipped Topping, page 170.

makes 12–14 biscuits
preparation time: 10 minutes
baking time: about 18 minutes
freezes well

PER BISCUIT: 110 calories, 3 g protein, 18 g carbohydrate, 3 g total fat (1 g sat fat, 1 g mono fat, 1 g poly fat), 4 mg cholesterol, 1 g dietary fiber, 17 RE vitamin A, < .5 mcg folate, < .5 mg vitamin C, 4 mg calcium, 1 mg iron, 33 mg potassium, 95 mg sodium

STRAWBERRY SHORTCAKE PER SERVING: 349 calories, 5 g protein, 20 g carbohydrate, 11 g total fat (6 g sat fat, 2 g mono fat, 1 g poly fat), 28 mg cholesterol, 3 g dietary fiber, 107 RE vitamin A, 26 mg vitamin C, 20 mg calcium, 2 mg iron, >77 mg potassium, 195 mg sodium

pancakes, crepes, cobblers & dumplings

granola snack
non-dairy

NEED SOMETHING more substantial than an apple to get you through the afternoon? A handful of this crunchy granola snack will keep you energized until dinner time.

1 ½ cups	large rolled oats	375 mL
½ cup	roasted soynuts	125 mL
1 cup	mixed nuts	250 mL
1 cup	wheat or rice cereal	250 mL
¼ cup, each,	soynut flakes, wheat germ, sesame seeds, shredded coconut, shelled sunflower seeds, and pumpkin seeds	60 mL
¼ cup	peanut butter or 2 tbsp. soynut butter + 2 tbsp. soy milk	60 mL
¼ cup	liquid honey	60 mL
2 tbsp.	soybean oil	30 mL
2 tbsp.	soy milk	30 mL
½ tsp.	ground cinnamon	2 mL
	pinch of nutmeg	

- Preheat oven to 325° F (165° C).
- In a large greased roasting pan, combine all dry ingredients.
- In a small bowl, mix together peanut butter, honey, oil, soy milk, cinnamon, and nutmeg until smooth. Drizzle over dry ingredients, then toss to coat.
- Bake about 15 minutes, stirring every 5 minutes for even browning. Remove from oven. Immediately spread granola on a large piece of wax paper or foil. Cool to room temperature. Store in airtight containers for up to 2 weeks.

makes about 7 cups
preparation time: 15 minutes
baking time: 15 minutes
freezes well;
when thawed, bake in 300° F (150° C) oven
for 10 minutes to regain crispness

PER ½ CUP: 271 calories, 13 g protein, 23 g carbohydrate, 16 g total fat (3 g sat fat, 1 g mono fat, 2 g poly fat), 6 g dietary fiber, 2 RE vitamin A, 18 mcg folate, < .5 mg vitamin C, 46 mg calcium, 2 mg iron, 91 mg potassium, 141 mg sodium

double chocolate chip cookies

(page 2)

blueberry cheesecake tart

(page 80)

tangy lemon cake

(page 55)

crème **caramel** à l'orange

(page 158)

cinnamon buns

(page 128)

strawberry shortcake
with **best whipped** topping *(page 100)*

plum coffee cake

(page 130)

pear and cherry crisp
with lemon sauce *(page 96)*

muffins, biscuits
& quick breads

blueberry muffins
non-dairy, 1-bowl recipe

THESE WONDERFUL blueberry muffins work well with liquid egg substitute, and since the liquid egg contains 80% less cholesterol than real eggs, you may occasionally choose to cook with it.

½ cup	soy flour	125 mL
1½ cups	unbleached flour	375 mL
2 tsp.	baking powder	10 mL
1 tsp.	baking soda	5 mL
½ tsp.	salt	2 mL
⅓–½ cup	sugar	75–125 mL
¼ cup	liquid egg	60 mL
1 cup	soy milk	250 mL
3 tbsp.	butter or margarine, melted	45 mL
3 tbsp.	unsweetened applesauce	45 mL
1 cup	blueberries, fresh or frozen *	250 mL

- Preheat oven to 425° F (215° C).
- Grease 12 medium muffin cups.
- In a large bowl, mix together dry ingredients. Make a hole in the center and add the liquid egg, soy milk, margarine, and applesauce. Stir until just combined. Gently fold in blueberries.
- Fill prepared muffin cups and bake for 15 minutes or until toothpick inserted in center comes out clean.

makes 12 medium muffins
preparation time: 10 minutes
baking time: 15 minutes
freezes well

*If using frozen berries, blend them into batter while still frozen. This will prevent them from coloring the batter purple.

PER MUFFIN: 131 calories, 5 g protein, 20 g carbohydrate, 3 g total fat (2 g sat fat, 1 g mono fat, < .5 g poly fat), 8 mg cholesterol, 1 g dietary fiber, 40 RE vitamin A, 2 mcg folate, 3 mg vitamin C, 5 mg calcium, 2 mg iron, 62 mg potassium, 228 mg sodium

I LOVE corn muffins, and although I don't eat them on a regular basis, for 2 weeks every winter when I'm in Florida, I have one every morning for breakfast.

1 cup	soy milk	250 mL
1 tbsp.	lemon juice	15 mL
1½ cups	cornmeal	375 mL
½ cup	unbleached flour	125 mL
¼ cup	soy flour	60 mL
⅓ cup	sugar	75 mL
½ tsp.	baking soda	2 mL
½ tsp.	salt	2 mL
½ cup	butter or margarine, melted	125 mL
1	egg	1
1	egg white	1

- Preheat oven to 375° F (190° C).
- Grease 12 medium muffin cups.
- In a large bowl, combine soy milk and lemon juice.
- In a medium bowl, combine cornmeal, flours, sugar, baking soda, and salt.
- Add melted butter, egg, and egg white to soy milk mixture. Beat until well blended. Gradually stir in flour mixture until the batter is smooth. Pour into prepared muffin cups. Bake for 20 minutes or until toothpick inserted in center comes out clean.

makes 12 medium muffins
preparation time: 15 minutes
baking time: 20 minutes
freezes well

VARIATION: For cornbread, bake the batter in a greased 9-inch (23 cm) square pan or 9-inch cast-iron skillet.

PER MUFFIN: 182 calories, 4 g protein, 22 g carbohydrate, 9 g total fat (5 g sat fat, 3 g mono fat, 1 g poly fat), 36 mg cholesterol, 1 g dietary fiber, 86 RE vitamin A, 6 mcg folate, 1 mg vitamin C, 6 mg calcium, 1 mg iron, 85 mg potassium, 150 mg sodium

banana oatmeal muffins

non-dairy, 1-bowl recipe

THESE MUFFINS are so popular at my daughter Bettina's house that she makes them at least once a month.

1 ¼ cups	rolled oats	310 mL
¼ cup	soy flour	60 mL
¾ cup	unbleached flour	175 mL
½ cup	sugar	125 mL
1 ½ tsp.	baking powder	7 mL
1 tsp.	baking soda	5 mL
¼ tsp.	salt	2 mL
1	egg, beaten	1
2 cups	mashed bananas	500 mL
¼ cup	soybean oil	60 mL
¼ cup	butter or margarine, melted	60 mL
¼ cup	raisins	60 mL
¼ cup	ground-roasted soynuts	60 mL

- Preheat oven to 375° F (190° C).
- Grease 10 to 12 medium muffin cups.
- In a large bowl, combine oats, flours, sugar, baking powder, baking soda, and salt. Stir in egg, mashed bananas, soybean oil, and melted butter. Fold in raisins and nuts. Pour into prepared muffin cups and bake for 20 to 25 minutes, or until toothpick inserted in center comes out clean.

makes 10 to 12 medium muffins
preparation time: 10 minutes
baking time: 20–25 minutes
freezes well

PER MUFFIN: 238 calories, 7 g protein, 33 g carbohydrate, 10 g total fat (3 g sat fat, 1 g mono fat, < .5 g poly fat), 26 mg cholesterol, 4 g dietary fiber, 46 RE vitamin A, 22 mcg folate, 4 mg vitamin C, 15 mg calcium, 1 mg iron, 180 mg potassium, 201 mg sodium

lemon cranberry muffins
non-dairy

SERVE THESE sweet and tangy muffins any time of day—for breakfast, brunch, or afternoon tea. The combination of soy milk, tofu, and soybean oil makes these extra moist.

2 cups	unbleached flour	500 mL
½ cup	soy flour	125 mL
1 tbsp.	baking powder	15 mL
½ tsp.	salt	2 mL
½ tsp.	cinnamon	2 mL
1	egg	1
1 cup	soy milk	250 mL
¼ cup	soft tofu	60 mL
⅓ cup	soybean oil	75 mL
¼ cup	liquid honey	60 mL
2 tsp.	grated lemon peel	10 mL
1½–2 cups	cranberries, fresh or frozen	375–500 mL

glaze

½ cup	confectioner's sugar	125 mL
1 tsp.	lemon peel	5 mL
2 tsp.	lemon juice	10 mL

- Preheat oven to 400° F (200° C). Grease 12 medium muffin cups.
- In a large bowl, mix together flours, baking powder, salt, and cinnamon.
- In a medium bowl, using an electric mixer or hand blender, blend together egg, soy milk, tofu, oil, honey, and lemon peel. Gradually stir into flour mixture until just combined; then fold in cranberries.
- Spoon batter into muffin cups and bake 5 minutes. Reduce oven temperature to 350° F (180° C) and bake an additional 20 minutes, or until toothpick inserted in center comes out clean.
- *For the glaze,* mix all ingredients together until smooth. Spoon over muffins while they are still warm.

makes 12 medium muffins
baking time: 20–25 minutes
freezes well

PER MUFFIN: 196 calories, 6 g protein, 28 g carbohydrate, 7 g total fat (1 g sat fat, < .5 g mono fat, < .5 g poly fat), 16 mg cholesterol, 2 g dietary fiber, 9 RE vitamin A, 2 mcg folate, 3 mg vitamin C, 7 mg calcium, 2 mg iron, 54 mg potassium, 179 mg sodium

honey lemon muffins
non-dairy, 1-bowl recipe

ALMOST EVERYONE loves a freshly baked muffin for breakfast; the honey-lemon glaze adds a tangy flavor to these delicious muffins.

1	egg	1
¼ cup	liquid honey	60 mL
¼ cup	soybean oil	60 mL
2 tsp.	grated lemon peel	10 mL
¾ cup	soy milk	175 mL
1½ cups	unbleached flour	375 mL
¼ cup	whole wheat flour	60 mL
¼ cup	soy flour	60 mL
2½ tsp.	baking powder	12 mL
¼ tsp.	salt	1 mL
½ tsp.	ground cinnamon	2 mL
	Honey Lemon Glaze, below	

- Preheat oven to 400° F (200° C). Line 12 medium muffin cups with paper baking cups.
- In a large bowl, beat together egg, honey, oil, and lemon peel. Stir in soy milk. Add dry ingredients, stirring just until flour is moistened.
- Fill muffin cups and bake about 20 minutes or until golden brown. Remove muffins from pan and drizzle glaze over them. Serve warm.

¼ cup	confectioner's sugar	60 mL
1 tbsp.	liquid honey	15 mL
2 tsp.	lemon juice	10 mL
2 tsp.	soy milk	10 mL
½ tsp.	grated lemon peel	2 mL

- In a small bowl, mix all ingredients until smooth.

makes 12 medium muffins
preparation time: muffins, 15 minutes
                    glaze, 5 minutes
freezes well

PER MUFFIN: 154 calories, 4 g protein, 23 g carbohydrate, 5 g total fat (1 g sat fat, < .5 g mono fat, < .5 g poly fat), 16 mg cholesterol, 1 g dietary fiber, 8 RE vitamin A, 2 mcg folate, 1 mg vitamin C, 4 mg calcium, 1 mg iron, 29 mg potassium, 116 mg sodium

applesauce and sour cream muffins

non-dairy, 1-bowl recipe

ALTHOUGH THE list of ingredients is rather long, these nutritious muffins take only minutes to prepare. Soy protein isolate provides a healthy dose of extra protein but no saturated fat or cholesterol.

¼ cup	packed brown sugar	60 mL
1	egg	1
2 tbsp.	soybean oil	30 mL
½ cup	soy sour cream	125 mL
½ cup	soft tofu	125 mL
1 tbsp.	lemon juice	15 mL
1 cup	unsweetened apple sauce	250 mL
1 cup	unbleached flour	250 mL
¼ cup	soy flour	60 mL
2 tbsp.	soy protein isolate (optional)	30 mL
1½ tsp.	baking powder	7 mL
½ tsp.	baking soda	2 mL
½ tsp.	ground cinnamon	2 mL
	pinch of salt	
¼ cup	raisins	60 mL
2 tbsp.	flaked or chopped Brazil nuts, or other nuts	30 mL

- Preheat oven to 375° F (190° C). Grease 8 large or 10 medium muffin cups.
- In a medium bowl, using an electric mixer or hand blender, blend together first 7 ingredients. Mix in next 7 ingredients until just combined. Fold in raisins and nuts. Spoon batter into muffin cups.
- Bake about 20 minutes, or until toothpick inserted in center comes out clean.

makes 8 large or 10 medium muffins
preparation time: 15 minutes
baking time: about 20 minutes
freezes well

PER MUFFIN: 164 calories, 5 g protein, 22 g carbohydrate, 7 g total fat (2 g sat fat, 1 g mono fat, 2 g poly fat), 19 mg cholesterol, 1 g dietary fiber, 14 RE vitamin A, 18 mcg folate, 11 mg vitamin C, 18 mg calcium, 1 mg iron, 117 mg potassium, 143 mg sodium

TO ADD extra soy protein to your diet, try these delicious and easy-to-make biscuits.

2 cups	unbleached flour	500 mL
¼ cup	soy flour	60 mL
¼ cup	whole wheat flour	60 mL
2 tbsp.	soy protein isolate	30 mL
1 tbsp.	baking powder	15 mL
1 tsp.	salt	5 mL
¼ cup	butter or margarine	60 mL
½ cup	soft tofu, mashed	125 mL
½ cup	soy milk	125 mL

- Preheat oven to 400° F (200° C).
- In a medium bowl, combine flours, soy protein, baking powder, and salt. Mix in butter with a pastry blender until mixture is evenly crumbled. Stir in tofu and soy milk. Knead a few seconds on a lightly floured surface until dough holds together. Roll or pat to ¾-inch (2cm) thickness. Cut into 2-inch (5cm) rounds with a cookie cutter and place rounds on an ungreased cookie sheet about 1 inch (2.5 cm) apart.
- Bake 18 to 20 minutes. Serve warm.

makes 12–14 biscuits
preparation time: 10 minutes
baking time: 18–20 minutes
freezes well

PER BISCUIT: 117 calories, 6 g protein, 15 g carbohydrate, 4 g total fat (2 g sat fat, 1 g mono fat, < .5 g poly fat), 9 mg cholesterol, 1 g dietary fiber, 32 RE vitamin A, 5 mcg folate, < .5 mg vitamin C, 9 mg calcium, 2 mg iron, 70 mg potassium, 256 mg sodium

quick 'n' easy carrot scones
non-dairy, 1-bowl recipe

ARE YOUR children not eating enough vegetables? I bet you won't have any trouble getting them to eat these nutritious carrot scones. They make a terrific after-school snack.

1 1/2 cups	unbleached flour	375 mL
1/4 cup	whole wheat flour	60 mL
1/4 cup	soy flour	60 mL
1/4 cup	granulated sugar	60 mL
2 1/2 tsp	baking powder	12 mL
	pinch of salt	
1/3 cup	butter or margarine	75 mL
3/4 to 1 cup	soy milk	175 mL–250 mL
1	egg, beaten	1
1 cup	shredded carrots	250 mL
1/4 to 1/2 cup	raisins	60–125 mL
	Cinnamon Glaze, below (optional)	

- Preheat oven to 400° F (200° C). In a large bowl, combine flours, sugar, baking powder, and salt. Mix in butter with a pastry blender until mixture is evenly crumbled. Stir in 3/4 cup (175mL) soy milk, egg, carrots, and raisins. If batter is too stiff, add remaining 1/4 cup (60mL) soy milk.
- Drop dough by heaping spoonfuls 2 inches (5 cm) apart on ungreased cookie sheet.
- Bake 15 to 18 minutes, or until light golden. Transfer scones to wire rack covered with wax paper (to catch the glaze drips) . Drizzle with Cinnamon Glaze, if desired. Serve warm.

***Note:** Leftover biscuits taste best when re-heated, either in a conventional oven, for a firm crust, or in a microwave oven, for a soft crust.

makes 10 to 12 scones
preparation time: 15 minutes
baking time: 15–18 minutes

¹/₄ cup	confectioner's sugar	60 mL
2 tsp.	soy milk	10 mL
¹/₄ tsp.	ground cinnamon	1 mL

• In a small bowl, mix all ingredients until smooth.

PER SCONE: 153 calories, 4 g protein, 21 g carbohydrate, 6 g total fat (3 g sat fat, 2 g mono fat, < .5 g poly fat), 29 mg cholesterol, 2 g dietary fiber, 313 RE vitamin A, 17 mcg folate, 1 mg vitamin C, 8 mg calcium, 1 mg iron, 83 mg potassium, 96 mg sodium

GLAZE PER SCONE: 10 calories, < .5 g protein, 3 g carbohydrate, < .5 g total fat (< .5 g poly fat), 29 mg cholesterol, < .5 mg dietary fiber, < .5 RE vitamin A, < .5 mcg folate, < .5 mg vitamin C, 1 mg calcium, < .5 mg iron, 1 mg potassium, < .5 mg sodium

yogurt soda bread
non-dairy, 1-bowl recipe

SURPRISE YOUR family by whipping up this tasty soy-rich quick bread in just a few minutes.

6 oz.	container vanilla soy yogurt	175 mL
¼ cup	vanilla soy milk	60 mL
1 tbsp.	lemon juice	15 mL
3 tbsp.	soybean oil	45 mL
1½ cups	unbleached flour	375 mL
¼ cup	soy flour	60 mL
1½ tsp.	baking powder	7 mL
¼ tsp.	baking soda	1 mL
¼ tsp.	salt	1 mL

- Preheat oven to 375° F (190° C). Grease a 9-inch (23 cm) round baking dish.
- In a large bowl, using an electric hand blender, blend together yogurt, soy milk, lemon juice, and oil. Gradually stir in dry ingredients. Knead dough just until it holds together. Pat dough to fit pan.
- Bake 20 to 25 minutes, or until light golden in color and toothpick inserted in center comes out clean. Cut into wedges. Serve warm.

makes 8 servings
preparation time: 10 minutes
baking time: 20–25 minutes

PER WEDGE: 151 calories, 5 g protein, 20 g carbohydrate, 6 g total fat (1 g sat fat, < .5 g mono fat, < .5 g poly fat), 1 g dietary fiber, < .5 RE vitamin A, < .5 mcg folate, 1 mg vitamin C, 3 mg calcium, 2 mg iron, 13 mg potassium, 195 mg sodium

banana bread
non-dairy

WHENEVER I have overripe bananas, I either freeze them in an airtight plastic container for later use or I make this delicious banana bread which also freezes well.

1 ⅓ cups	unbleached flour	325 mL
⅓ cup	whole wheat flour	75 mL
⅓ cup	soy flour	75 mL
2 tsp.	baking powder	10 mL
½ tsp.	baking soda	2 mL
¼ tsp.	salt	1 mL
4	medium overripe bananas	4
1	egg, beaten	1
½ cup	granulated sugar	125 mL
¼ cup	soybean oil	60 mL
6 tbsp.	soy milk	90 mL
2 tbsp.	fresh lemon juice	30 mL

- Preheat oven to 350° F (180° C). Grease a 9 x 5-inch (23 x 13 cm) loaf pan.
- In a large bowl, combine flours, baking powder, baking soda, and salt.
- In a medium bowl, mash bananas. Mix in remaining ingredients. Fold mixture into dry ingredients until just combined.
- Pour batter into pan and bake 50 to 60 minutes, or until toothpick inserted in center comes out clean. Let stand 10 minutes, then remove from pan and let cool on wire rack.

makes 12–14 servings
preparation time: 20 minutes
baking time: approximately 1 hour
freezes well

PER SERVING: 158 calories, 4 g protein, 26 g carbohydrate, 5 g total fat (1 g sat fat, < .5 g mono fat, < .5 g poly fat), 13 mg cholesterol, 2 g dietary fiber, 9 RE vitamin A, 8 mcg folate, 4 mg vitamin C, 4 mg calcium, 1 mg iron, 149 mg potassium, 118 mg sodium

flax, banana, and orange bread
non-dairy

FLAX SEEDS are rich in Omega-3 polyunsaturated fatty acids, essential nutrients for maintaining good health and normal growth. These seeds combined with potassium-rich bananas make for a nutritious and tasty quick bread.

1 cup	unbleached flour	250 mL
½ cup	whole wheat flour	125 mL
¼ cup	soy flour	60 mL
2½ tsp.	baking powder	12 mL
½ tsp.	baking soda	2 mL
½ tsp.	ground cinnamon	2 mL
⅓ cup	granulated sugar	75 mL
	pinch of salt	
¼ cup	flax seeds	60 mL
¼ cup	chopped nuts	60 mL
2	medium ripe bananas, mashed	2
1	egg	1
1	egg white	1
½ cup	soft or medium tofu	125 mL
1 tbsp.	frozen orange juice concentrate	15 mL
3 tbsp.	soybean oil	45 mL

- Preheat oven to 350° F (180° C). Grease a 9 x 5-inch (23 x 13 cm) loaf pan.
- In a large bowl, sift together flours, baking powder, baking soda, and cinnamon. Add sugar, salt, flax seeds, and nuts.
- In a medium bowl, with a hand blender, blend together remaining ingredients until smooth. Mix into dry ingredients to make a thick batter. Spread batter evenly in pan.
- Bake 40 to 50 minutes or until toothpick inserted in center comes out clean. Let stand 5 minutes, then turn out onto wire rack to cool.

makes 12–14 servings
preparation time: 15 minutes
baking time: 40–50 minutes
freezes well

PER SERVING: 153 calories, 5 g protein, 21 g carbohydrate, 6 g total fat (1 g sat fat, 1 g mono fat, 2 g poly fat), 13 mg cholesterol, 2 g dietary fiber, 9 RE vitamin A, 17 mcg folate, 3 mg vitamin C, 15 mg calcium, 1 mg iron, 129 mg potassium, 92 mg sodium

strawberry quick bread

LOTS OF soy and other nutritious ingredients are part of this delicious moist quick bread.

2¹⁄₂ cups	unbleached flour	625 mL
¹⁄₂ cup	soy flour	125 mL
1¹⁄₂ tsp.	baking soda	7 mL
¹⁄₂ tsp.	salt	2 mL
1¹⁄₂ cups	granulated sugar	375 mL
2	eggs, beaten	2
2	egg whites	2
¹⁄₄ cup	soybean oil	60 mL
2	6-oz. containers strawberry soy yogurt or regular strawberry yogurt	2 x 175 mL
¹⁄₄ cup	toasted soy flakes	60 mL
2 cups	fresh sliced strawberries	500 mL

- Grease two 8 x 4-inch (20 x 10 cm) loaf pans.
- Preheat oven to 350° F (180° C).
- In a large bowl, blend all ingredients, except strawberries, until smooth; then fold in strawberries. Pour batter into prepared pans.
- Bake 40 to 50 minutes, or until toothpick inserted in center comes out clean. Let stand 5 minutes, then turn out onto wire rack to cool.

makes 2 loaves, 10–12 servings each
preparation time: 15 minutes
baking time: 40–50 minutes
freezes well

VARIATIONS: Instead of strawberries, try other berries or chopped up fruit.

PER SERVING: 148 calories, 5 g protein, 25 g carbohydrate, 3 g total fat (< .5 g sat fat, < .5 g mono fat, < .5 g poly fat), 16 mg cholesterol, 1 g dietary fiber, 7 RE vitamin A, 4 mcg folate, 8 mg vitamin C, 4 mg calcium, 1 mg iron, 32 mg potassium, 116 mg sodium

applesauce loaf

non-dairy, 1-bowl recipe

A HEALTHY snack, perfect for kids' lunch boxes or a picnic. The protein-rich soy flakes add a nutty flavor to this bread.

¼ cup	butter or margarine, softened	60 mL
¼ cup	soft tofu	60 mL
¾ cup	packed brown sugar	175 mL
1	egg	1
1 cup	unsweetened applesauce	250 mL
1½ cups	unbleached flour	375 mL
¼ cup	soy flour	60 mL
¼ cup	wheat germ	60 mL
	pinch of salt	
1 tsp.	baking soda	5 mL
½ tsp.	baking powder	2 mL
1 tsp.	ground cinnamon	5 mL
¼ tsp.	ground cloves	1 mL
⅓ cup	raisins	75 mL
2 tbsp.	toasted soy flakes (optional)	30 mL

- Preheat oven to 350° F (180° C). Grease a 9 x 5-inch (23 x 13 cm) loaf pan.
- In a large bowl, cream together butter, tofu, and sugar. Beat in egg and applesauce. Stir in next 8 ingredients. When smooth, fold in raisins and soy flakes, if using. Spread batter evenly in pan.
- Bake 1 hour, or until toothpick inserted in center comes out clean. Let stand 10 minutes. Loosen sides of loaf with a knife and turn out onto wire rack to cool.

makes 12–14 servings
preparation: 15 minutes
baking: 1 hour
freezes well

PER SERVING: 158 calories, 4 g protein, 28 g carbohydrate, 4 g total fat (2 g sat fat, 1 g mono fat, < .5 g poly fat), 22 mg cholesterol, 1 g dietary fiber, 37 RE vitamin A, 24 mcg folate, 7 mg vitamin C, 19 mg calcium, 2 mg iron, 121 mg potassium, 80 mg sodium

quick health loaf

non-dairy

THIS WHOLESOME loaf requires no rising time which makes it a snap to prepare. Great with a little butter or cheese.

½ cup	raisins	125 mL
1 cup	rolled oats	250 mL
1 cup	boiling water	250 mL
1	egg, beaten	1
¼ cup	packed brown sugar	60 mL
¼ cup	soy milk	60 mL
½ cup	soft tofu	125 mL
1 tsp.	lemon juice	5 mL
1 cup	unbleached flour	250 mL
¼ cup	soy flour	60 mL
½ cup	wheat bran	125 mL
2 tbsp.	wheat germ	30 mL
2 tsp.	baking soda	10 mL
½ tsp.	salt	2 mL
2 tbsp.	toasted soy flakes	30 mL

- Preheat oven to 350° F (180° C). Grease a 9 x 5-inch (23 x 13 cm) loaf pan.
- In a medium bowl, combine raisins and oats. Pour boiling water over them. Set aside.
- In a large bowl, blend egg, sugar, soy milk, tofu, and lemon juice. Stir in remaining dry ingredients. When smooth, fold in raisin and oat mixture. Spread batter in pan.
- Bake about 45 minutes or until toothpick inserted in center comes out clean. Let stand 5 minutes, then turn out onto wire rack to cool.

makes 12–14 servings
preparation time: 15 minutes
baking time: 45 minutes
freezes well

PER SERVING: 121 calories, 5 g protein, 22 g carbohydrate, 2 g total fat (< .5 g sat fat, < .5 g mono fat, < .5 g poly fat), 13 mg cholesterol, 2 g dietary fiber, 7 RE vitamin A, 29 mcg folate, < .5 mg vitamin C, 12 mg calcium, 1 mg iron, 103 mg potassium, 210 mg sodium

pineapple cranberry loaf
non-dairy

I LOVE the taste and texture of chunks of fruit baked into soft breads and muffins. The winning combination of pineapple and cranberries gives this loaf a flavorful tang. Even if you typically cook and bake with fresh fruit, don't hesitate to use canned pineapple, which is just as good as fresh and is cheaper, available year-round, and takes less time to prepare.

¾ cup	granulated sugar	175 mL
3 tbsp.	soybean oil	45 mL
1	egg	1
¼ cup	soft tofu	60 mL
8 oz.	(can) pineapple tidbits, with juice	227 mL
1½ cups	unbleached flour	375 mL
½ cup	soy flour	125 mL
1½ tsp.	baking powder	7 mL
½ tsp.	baking soda	2 mL
¼ tsp.	salt	1 mL
1 cup	fresh or frozen cranberries, coarsely chopped	250 mL
1–2 tbsp.	toasted soy flakes	15–30 mL

- Preheat oven to 350° F (180° C). Grease a 9 x 5-inch (23 x 13 cm) loaf pan.
- In a large bowl, using an electric mixer or hand blender, blend together sugar, oil, egg, tofu, and pineapple juice. Gradually stir in flours, baking powder, baking soda, and salt. Fold in pineapple, cranberries, and soy flakes. Transfer to prepared pan.
- Bake 50 to 60 minutes until lightly browned, or until toothpick inserted in center comes out clean. Let stand 5 minutes, then turn out onto wire rack to cool.

makes 12–14 servings
preparation time: 15 minutes
baking time: 50–60 minutes
freezes well

PER SERVING: 148 calories, 5 g protein, 25 g carbohydrate, 4 g total fat (1 g sat fat, < .5 g mono fat, < .5 g poly fat), 13 mg cholesterol, 1 g dietary fiber, 7 RE vitamin A, 2 mcg folate, 3 mg vitamin C, 6 mg calcium, 1 mg iron, 38 mg potassium, 108 mg sodium

cherry and lime pound cake

SWEET CHERRIES and sour lime juice combine with low-fat tofu and soy milk to make a flavorful cake.

½ cup	sugar	125 mL
¼ cup	butter or margarine, softened	60 mL
½ cup	soft or medium tofu	125 mL
2	eggs	2
½ cup	vanilla soy milk	125 mL
2 tsp.	lime juice	10 mL
2 tsp.	grated lime peel	10 mL
2¼ cups	unbleached flour, sifted	560 mL
¼ cup	soy flour, sifted	60 mL
1 tsp.	baking soda	5 mL
¼ tsp.	salt	1 mL
¾ cup	dried Bing Cherries	175 mL
2 tbsp.	coarsely chopped honey-roasted soynuts (optional)	30 mL

- Preheat oven to 350° F (180° C). Grease an 8 x 4-inch (20 x 10 cm) loaf pan.
- In a large bowl, using an electric mixer or hand blender, beat sugar, butter, and tofu until smooth. Beat in eggs, soy milk, lime juice, and peel. Blend in flours, baking soda, and salt. When smooth, fold in cherries. Spread batter in pan and sprinkle with soynuts, if desired. Bake 1 hour or until toothpick inserted in center comes out clean. Let stand 5 minutes, then turn out onto wire rack to cool.

makes 10–12 servings
preparation time: 15 minutes
baking time: 1 hour
freezes well

PER SERVING: 218 calories, 6 g protein, 37 g carbohydrate, 6 g total fat (3 g sat fat, 2 g mono fat, 1 g poly fat), 42 mg cholesterol, 3 g dietary fiber, 65 RE vitamin A, 7 mcg folate, 5 mg vitamin C, 19 mg calcium, 2 mg iron, 199 mg potassium, 130 mg sodium

almond pound cake
non-dairy, 1-bowl recipe

IF YOU'RE serving afternoon tea or coffee, be sure to include this mild flavored almond cake. Other glazes such as lemon or caramel go well with this cake, too.

¼ cup	butter or margarine, softened	60 mL
2 tbsp.	soybean oil	30 mL
½ cup	granulated sugar	125 mL
¼ cup	liquid honey	60 mL
½ cup	vanilla soy milk	125 mL
½ cup	soft or medium tofu	125 mL
1	egg	1
1	egg white	1
¼ tsp.	almond extract	1 mL
1½ cups	unbleached flour	375 mL
¼ cup	soy flour	60 mL
2 tsp.	baking powder	10 mL
	pinch of salt	
¼ cup	slivered almonds (optional)	60 mL
	Almond Glaze, below	

- Preheat oven to 350° F (180° C). Grease a 9 x 5-inch (23 x 13 cm) loaf pan.
- In a large bowl, using an electric mixer or hand blender, beat first 9 ingredients until smooth. Fold in remaining ingredients. Transfer batter to pan.
- Bake about 60 minutes, or until toothpick inserted in center comes out clean. Cool 15 minutes, then turn cake out onto a wire rack covered with wax paper (to catch the glaze drips). Spoon glaze over cake. Cool completely.

½ cup	confectioner's sugar	125 mL
3–4 tsp.	soy milk	15–20 mL
¼ tsp.	almond extract	1 mL

- In a small bowl, mix all ingredients until smooth. If too thick, add a little soy milk. If too thin, add extra confectioner's sugar.

makes 12–14 servings
preparation time: cake, 15 minutes
glaze, 5 minutes
baking time: about 60 minutes
freezes well

PER SERVING: 173 calories, 4 g protein, 26 g carbohydrate, 6 g total fat (2 g sat fat, 1 g mono fat, < .5 g poly fat), 22 mg cholesterol, 1 g dietary fiber, 38 RE vitamin A, 2 mcg folate, < .5 mg vitamin C, 6 mg calcium, 1 mg iron, 40 mg potassium, 52 mg sodium

lemony cranberry bundt cake

non-dairy, 1-bowl recipe

FRIENDS AND family will enjoy this cake when they drop in for a little Christmas cheer during the holiday season. If you prefer, you can bake it in two 8 x 4-inch (20 x 10 cm) loaves.

¾ cup	butter or margarine, softened	175 mL
1 cup	granulated sugar	250 mL
2	eggs	2
2	egg whites	2
½ cup	soft tofu	125 mL
1 tbsp.	grated lemon peel	15 mL
1 tbsp.	fresh lemon juice	15 mL
2½ cups	unbleached flour	625 mL
½ cup	soy flour	125 mL
2 tsp.	baking powder	10 mL
½ tsp.	salt	2 mL
1 cup	vanilla soy milk	250 mL
1 cup	dried cranberries	250 mL
	Glaze, below	

½ cup	confectioner's sugar	125 mL
2 tbsp.	lemon juice	30 mL

- Grease a 10-inch (25 cm) bundt or tube pan. Preheat oven to 325° F (165° C).
- In a large bowl, using an electric mixer or hand blender, beat first seven ingredients until smooth.
- Gradually add dry ingredients, alternating with soy milk, until just combined. Fold in cranberries.
- Spoon batter into prepared pan and bake 50 to 60 minutes, or until toothpick inserted in center comes out clean.
- For the glaze, combine confectioner's sugar and lemon juice in a small bowl until smooth. Pierce 15 to 20 holes in top of hot cake with a toothpick and spoon glaze over it. Let cool in pan on wire rack.

makes 20–22 servings
preparation time: 20 minutes
baking time: 50–60 minutes
freezes well

PER SERVING: 189 calories, 4 g protein, 28 g carbohydrate, 7 g total fat (4 g sat fat, 2 g mono fat, < .5 g poly fat), 34 mg cholesterol, 2 g dietary fiber, 69 RE vitamin A, 3 mcg folate, 6 mg vitamin C, 10 mg calcium, 1 mg iron, 68 mg potassium, 93 mg sodium

yeast breads

cinnamon buns
non-dairy

BECAUSE THESE freeze well, you might consider making a batch to have on hand as a breakfast treat. In our family we all love yeast breads and these low-fat cinnamon buns created by my daughter Bettina are everybody's favorite.

1 cup	soy milk, scalded	250 mL
¼ cup	butter or margarine	60 mL
½ cup	sugar	125 mL
1 tsp.	salt	5 mL
¼ cup	lukewarm water	60 mL
1 tsp.	honey	5 mL
2 tbsp.	(2 packets) active dry yeast	30 mL
3	eggs	3
1 cup	soft tofu	250 mL
2 tsp.	grated lemon peel	10 mL
1 cup	soy flour	250 mL
4–5 cups	unbleached flour	1–1.25 kg

filling

⅓ cup	brown sugar	75 mL
⅓ cup	granulated sugar	75 mL
2 tbsp.	cinnamon	30 mL
2 tbsp.	butter or margarine, melted	30 mL
½ cup	raisins and/or nuts (optional)	125 mL

- In a large bowl, pour hot soy milk over butter, sugar, and salt. Pour lukewarm water into a small bowl. Stir in honey and yeast. Let stand 10 minutes, or until yeast is bubbly; then stir.
- In a separate bowl, combine eggs and tofu with a whisk or hand blender until smooth.
- When the milk mixture has cooled to lukewarm, stir in yeast, egg, tofu mixture, and lemon peel. Gradually blend in flours to make a soft dough. Turn out onto floured surface and knead until smooth and elastic, about 5 minutes. Form into a ball and place in a lightly greased bowl, turning to grease top. Cover and let rise in warm place, free from draft, until doubled in bulk, about 1 hour.
- To make the filling, combine in a small bowl, the sugars and cinnamon. On floured surface, roll out dough into a 24 x 15-inch (60 x 38 cm) rectangle. Brush with melted butter and sprinkle evenly with cinnamon mixture and raisins and/or nuts, if using. Carefully roll up the dough and gently pinch the seam. Cut into 24 1-inch (2.5 cm) slices. Place side by side, cut side down, in 2 greased 9 x 13-inch (23 x 33 cm) baking pans. Cover and let rise until doubled in bulk, about 1 hour.
- Bake at 350° F (180° C) for 15 to 20 minutes, or until lightly browned and a toothpick inserted in center comes out clean. Cool on wire rack.

makes 24 buns
preparation time: 40 minutes
rising time: 2 hours
baking time: 15–20 minutes

PER BUN: 163 calories, 6 g protein, 26 g carbohydrate, 4 g total fat (2 g sat fat, 1 g mono fat, < .5 g poly fat), 31 mg cholesterol, 1 g dietary fiber, 39 RE vitamin A, 26 mcg folate, < .5 mg vitamin C, 17 mg calcium, 2 mg iron, 73 mg potassium, 109 mg sodium

plum coffee cake
non-dairy

THIS LIGHTLY sweetened yeast coffee cake is as easy to make as a quick bread since it requires no kneading.

¹/₂ cup	warm water	125 mL
1 tsp.	honey	5 mL
1 tbsp.	(1 packet) active dry yeast	15 mL
¹/₂ cup	soy milk, scalded	125 mL
2 tbsp.	butter or margarine	30 mL
¹/₄ cup	sugar	60 mL
¹/₂ tsp.	salt	2 mL
1	egg, beaten	1
1¹/₂ cups	unbleached flour	375 mL
¹/₄ cup	soy flour	60 mL
1¹/₂ cups	ripe chopped plums	375 mL
2–3 tbsp.	brown sugar (depending on tartness of plums)	30–45 mL
	ground cinnamon, to taste	
2 tsp.	butter, to dot plums, optional	10 mL

- Grease a 9-inch (23 cm) square pan. Pour lukewarm water into a small bowl. Stir in honey and yeast. Let stand 10 minutes or until yeast is bubbly.
- Meanwhile, in a medium bowl, pour hot soy milk over butter, sugar, and salt. Stir to melt butter. When cooled to lukewarm, stir in yeast and egg. Gradually mix in flours to form a smooth thick batter.
- Spread batter evenly in pan. Top with plums; sprinkle with brown sugar and cinnamon. Dot with butter, if desired. Cover and let rise in warm place, free from draft, until doubled in bulk, about 1 hour.
- Bake at 375° F (190° C) for 20 to 25 minutes or until crust is lightly browned and plums are soft. Cool on wire rack.

makes 9 servings
preparation time: 20 minutes
rising time: 1 hour
baking time: 20–25 minutes
freezes well

VARIATIONS: Try with other fruits, such as apples, pears, or cherries.

PER SERVING: 159 calories, 5 g protein, 27 g carbohydrate, 3 g total fat (2 g sat fat, 1 g mono fat, < .5 g poly fat), 28 mg cholesterol, 1 g dietary fiber, 34 RE vitamin A, 34 mcg folate, 3 mg vitamin C, 11 mg calcium, 2 mg iron, 77 mg potassium, 143 mg sodium

raisin casserole bread

AN ABUNDANCE of soy in the form of soy flour, tofu, and soy milk does not alter the original pleasing taste and texture of traditional raisin breads. Enjoy it for breakfast or afternoon tea.

2 tsp.	honey	10 mL
¾ cup	warm water	175 mL
2 tbsp.	(2 packets) active dry yeast	30 mL
¾ cup	soy milk	175 mL
3 tbsp.	butter or margarine, cut up	45 mL
½ cup	granulated sugar	125 mL
1 tsp.	salt	5 mL
½ cup	soft tofu	125 mL
1	egg	1
1 tsp.	grated lemon peel	5 mL
½ cup	soy flour	125 mL
3½–4 cups	unbleached flour	875–1000 mL
½–¾ cup	raisins	125–175 mL

- In a large bowl, dissolve honey in warm water. Sprinkle yeast over it and let stand 10 minutes, or until mixture is bubbly; then stir.
- Meanwhile, in a medium saucepan, heat soy milk, butter, sugar, and salt over low heat until butter has melted.★ Remove from heat.
- In a small bowl, with an electric hand blender, blend together tofu, egg, and grated peel. Mix into soy milk mixture, then stir into dissolved yeast. Gradually add flours, beating to make a smooth stiff batter. Cover and let rise in warm place, free from draft, until doubled in bulk, about 1 hour.
- Stir batter down; beat in raisins until they are evenly distributed, about 30 seconds. Divide batter between 2 greased 1-quart (1.5 L) casseroles or pour into 1 3-quart (4.5 L) casserole. (A 10-inch [25 cm] springform pan works well, too.) Let rise until doubled in bulk, about 40 minutes.
- Bake smaller loaves in 350° F (180° C) oven for 35 to 40 minutes, or until they are evenly browned. Bake the large loaf 5 to 7 minutes longer. Remove from pans and cool on wire racks.

*Can also be heated in microwave oven.

Makes 20–24 servings
Preparation time: 30 minutes
Rising time: first rise, 60 minutes
second rise, 40 minutes
Baking time: small loaves, 35–40 minutes
large loaf, 40–50 minutes

PER SLICE: 118 calories, 4 g protein, 21 g carbohydrate, 2 g total fat (1 g sat fat, 1 g mono fat, < .5 poly fat), 12 mg cholesterol, 1 g dietary fiber, 18 RE vitamin A, 38 mcg folate, < .5 mg vitamin C, 6 mg calcium, 2 mg iron, 70 mg potassium, 103 mg sodium

stollen

non-dairy

THIS TRADITIONAL German Christmas bread has become popular in North America and can be found in many bakeries, delis, and supermarkets. This homemade version is delicious. Serve it Christmas morning while you and your family are opening presents.

1 cup	hot soy milk	250 mL
½ cup	butter or margarine, cubed	125 mL
½ cup	sugar	125 mL
½ tsp.	salt	2 mL
1 cup	lukewarm water	250 mL
2 tsp.	honey	10 mL
2 tbsp.	(2 packets) active dry yeast	30 mL
2	eggs, beaten	2
½ cup	soy flour	125 mL
4½–5½ cups	unbleached flour	1–1½ kg
¾ cup	slivered almonds	175 mL
½ cup	chopped dried citrus peel	125 mL
½ cup	raisins	125 mL
	confectioner's sugar, for sprinkling	

- In a large bowl, pour hot soy milk over butter, sugar, and salt.
- In a small bowl, combine lukewarm water with honey. Sprinkle yeast over water and let stand 10 minutes, or until mixture is bubbly; then stir.
- Stir eggs into soy milk mixture, then stir in dissolved yeast. Gradually blend in flours to make a soft dough. Turn out onto floured surface and knead until smooth and elastic, about 5 minutes. Knead in almonds, chopped dried citrus peel, and raisins until they are evenly distributed in dough. Form into a ball and place in greased bowl, turning to grease top. Cover and let rise in a warm place, free from draft, until doubled in bulk, about 1 hour.
- Punch dough down; transfer to floured surface. Cut dough in half and shape each half into a 14 x 9-inch (36 x 23 cm) oval. Fold in half lengthwise. Place both stollen on a large greased baking sheet 4 inches (10 cm) apart. Cover and let rise until doubled in bulk, about 1 hour.
- Bake at 350° F (180° C) about 30 minutes or until lightly browned. Remove from baking sheet and cool on wire racks. Sprinkle liberally with confectioner's sugar while still warm.

makes 2 large stollen, about 22 slices each
preparation time: 30 minutes
rising time: about 2 hours
baking time: 30 minutes
freezes well

PER SLICE: 104 calories, 3 g protein, 16 g carbohydrate, 3 g total fat (1 g sat fat, 1 g mono fat, < .5 g poly fat), 14 mg cholesterol, 1 g dietary fiber, 31 RE vitamin A, 22 mcg folate, < .5 mg vitamin C, 9 mg calcium, 1 mg iron, 75 mg potassium, 32 mg sodium

caribbean holiday sweet bread

BAKING THIS festive yeast bread for two hours in a slow oven gives it a moist cake-like consistency. I have considerably reduced the sugar, shortening, and egg content called for in the original recipe while adding healthy soy ingredients.

1 tbsp.	granulated sugar	15 mL
1 cup	warm soy milk	250 mL
½ cup	warm water	125 mL
1½ tbsp.	(1½ packets) active dry yeast	12 g
5 cups	unbleached flour, divided	1.25 kg
1 cup	soy flour	250 mL
2 tsp.	grated orange peel	10 mL
½ tsp.	ground cinnamon	2 mL
½ tsp.	ground cloves	2 mL
1¾ cups	granulated sugar	425 mL
¼ cup	butter or margarine, melted	60 mL
¼ cup	soybean oil	60 mL
2	eggs, beaten	2
½–¾ cup	soy milk, at room temperature	125–175 mL
½ cup	raisins	125 mL
½ cup	pitted prunes, chopped	125 mL
2 tbsp.	chopped dried citrus peel	30 mL
2 tbsp.	ground almonds	30 mL
2 tbsp.	toasted soy flakes	30 mL
¼ cup	eau-de-vie (such as prune or kirsch)	60 mL
8	whole almonds, as a garnish	8

- In a large bowl, dissolve 1 tbsp. (15 mL) sugar in warm soy milk and warm water. Sprinkle yeast over this mixture and let stand 10 minutes, or until yeast is bubbly; then stir.
- Gradually add 1 cup (250 mL) unbleached flour and 1 cup (250 mL) soy flour to yeast mixture, beating to make a smooth stiff batter. Stir in orange peel, cinnamon, and cloves. Cover and let rise in warm place, free from draft, until doubled in bulk, about 1 hour 30 minutes.
- Sift together 1¾ cups (425mL) sugar and remaining 4 cups (600g) of flour.
- Stir melted butter, oil, and eggs into yeast mixture. Gradually add remaining soy milk, alternating with sugar and flour mixture. Beat until batter is thick and smooth; then fold in remaining ingredients, except for the whole almonds.
- Preheat oven to 300° F (150° C).
- Transfer batter to a greased 9- or 10-inch (23 or 25 cm) springform pan. Decorate top with almonds. Let rise another 45 minutes.
- Bake about 2 hours, or until toothpick inserted in center comes out clean. Loosely cover with foil if cake gets dark. Cool for 10 minutes, unmold and cool on wire rack.

makes 1 large loaf or 20–24 servings
preparation time: 40 minutes
rising time: first rise, 1 hour 30 minutes
second rise, 45 minutes
baking time: about 2 hours

PER SERVING: 239 calories, 7 g protein, 39 g carbohydrate, 6 g total fat (2 g sat fat, 1 g mono fat, < .5 g poly fat), 21 mg cholesterol, 2 g dietarey fiber, 27 RE vitamin A, 16 mcg folate, 1 mg vitamin C, 10 mg calcium, 2 mg iron, 78 mg potassium, 10 mg sodium

bagels
non-dairy

MAKING BAGELS isn't as difficult as you might think, though the formed bagels must be boiled before they're baked. Not too many home bakers bake their own bagels, but if you're in the mood for a wholesome, fresh, out-of-the-oven doughy bagel, then this recipe (adapted by my daughter Bettina) is worth making.

1 tsp.	honey	5 mL
½ cup	warm water	125 mL
1 tbsp.	(1 packet) active dry yeast	15 mL
1½ cups	warm water	375 mL
3 tbsp.	sugar	45 mL
1 tbsp.	salt	15 mL
¼ cup	soft tofu, mashed	60 mL
4–4½ cups	unbleached flour	1–1.1 kg
½ cup	soy flour	125 mL
1	egg white	1
1 tbsp.	cold water	15 mL
1 tbsp.	crushed soynuts or sesame seeds (optional)	

- In a large bowl, dissolve honey in ½ cup (125 mL) warm water. Sprinkle yeast over it and let stand 10 minutes, or until yeast is bubbly; then stir.
- Meanwhile, in a small bowl, combine 1½ cups (375 mL) warm water, sugar, and salt. Whisk in mashed tofu. Add to dissolved yeast. Stir in 1½ cups (375 mL) unbleached flour. Gradually add remaining flours to form a soft dough. Turn out onto a floured surface and knead until smooth and elastic, about 5 minutes. Place in ungreased bowl, cover and let rise in warm place, free from draft, about 20 minutes.
- Punch dough down, then turn out onto lightly floured surface. Divide dough into 12 equal parts; shape into balls; punch out 1-inch (2.5 cm) centers (a small cookie cutter works well). Place on ungreased baking sheet, cover and let rise 20 to 30 minutes.
- In a large pot, bring 3 inches (7.5 cm) of water to a boil. Using a large, flat slotted spoon, add a few bagels at a time and let simmer for 7 minutes. Remove from water and place on a dish towel. Cool for 5 minutes, then transfer to ungreased or parchment-lined baking sheet.

the soy dessert & baking book

- In a small bowl, combine egg white with 1 tbsp. (15 mL) cold water.
- Bake at 375° F (190° C) for 10 minutes. Brush with egg white mixture and sprinkle with soynuts if using. Bake another 20 minutes. Remove from baking sheet and let cool on wire rack.

makes 12 bagels
preparation time: 30 minutes
rising time: 50 minutes
cooking time: in boiling water, 7 minutes per batch
in oven, 30 minutes

PER BAGEL: 166 calories, 7 g protein, 34 g carbohydrate, < .5 g total fat (< .5 g sat fat, < .5 g mono fat), 2 g dietary fiber, < .5 RE vitamin A, 23 mcg folate, < .5 vitamin C, 2 mg calcium, 3 mg iron, 29 mg potassium, 588 mg sodium

hot & cold puddings

irish cream chocolate pudding

non-dairy, 1-bowl recipe

IF YOU'RE in the mood for a rich chocolatey dessert, this is the one for you!
I've replaced all the milk and cream with chocolate soy milk.

2 tbsp.	granulated sugar	30 mL
¼ cup	cornstarch	60 mL
2 cups	chocolate soy milk*	500 mL
1	egg yolk	1
⅓ cup	Irish cream or other liqueur	75 mL
2 oz.	semi-sweet chocolate, coarsely chopped	56 g
	chocolate curls for garnish (optional)	

- In a medium saucepan, combine sugar and cornstarch. Whisk in soy milk and egg yolk.
- Over medium heat, whisk constantly until mixture is just thickened. Remove from heat; whisk in Irish cream. Stir in chocolate until melted.
- Pour pudding into five individual serving bowls. Place plastic wrap on surface of each to prevent a skin from forming. Chill until ready to serve. Garnish with chocolate curls,★★ if desired.

makes 5 servings
preparation time: 10 minutes
cooking time: 5 minutes
chilling time: 1 hour or more

*or 2 cups (500 mL) soy milk and 4 tbsp (60 mL) instant hot chocolate mix.

PER SERVING: 216 calories, 4 g protein, 26 g carbohydrate, 7 g total fat (1 g sat fat, 1 g mono fat, 1 g poly fat), 43 mg cholesterol, 1 g dietary fiber, 22 RE vitamin A, 6 mcg folate, 9 mg calcium, 1 mg iron, 147 mg potassium, 16 mg sodium

**see page 53

rice pudding with white chocolate

THE ADDITION of white chocolate gives this traditional dessert a lovely creamy texture as well as delicious flavor. A great make-ahead dessert.

1 cup	water	250 mL
1/2 cup	short grain white rice	125 mL
2 tbsp.	sugar	30 mL
3 cups	vanilla soy milk	750 mL
1/4–1/2 cup	raisins	60–125 mL
2 oz.	white chocolate, chopped	60 g
	ground cinnamon, to taste	
	shredded coconut, as a garnish, to taste	

- In a large saucepan, bring water to a boil. Stir in rice, cover, and, over low heat, cook rice until water is almost absorbed, about 10 minutes. Stir in sugar, soy milk, and raisins. Bring to a boil, cover, and simmer another 30 to 40 minutes, or until rice is soft and pudding is creamy. Remove from heat; stir in chopped chocolate.
- Divide pudding among 6 individual bowls. Sprinkle with cinnamon and shredded coconut, if desired. Serve warm or cold.

makes 6 servings
preparation time: 10 minutes
cooking time: 40–50 minutes

PER SERVING: 194 calories, 5 g protein, 31 g carbohydrate, 5 g total fat ($<$ .5 g sat fat, $<$ .5 g mono fat, 1 g poly fat), 3 g dietary fiber, 4 RE vitamin A, 67 mcg folate, $<$ .5 vitamin C, 9 mg calcium, 2 mg iron, 272 mg potassium, 22 mg sodium

vanilla soy pudding
non-dairy, 1-bowl recipe

LIGHTLY FLAVORED and smoothly textured, this nutritious vanilla pudding is ideal for young children.

¹/₄ cup	water	60 mL
1 tbsp.	(1 packet) unflavored gelatin	15 mL
1³/₄ cups	vanilla soy milk	425 mL
2 tbsp.	sugar	30 mL

- Pour water into a small saucepan. Sprinkle gelatin over water. Heat over low heat until gelatin is dissolved.
- Meanwhile, in a medium saucepan, bring soy milk and sugar to a boil. Stir in dissolved gelatin. Pour into individual bowls. Cool to room temperature, cover, and chill until set, about 2 hours.
- Serve as is, or loosen pudding by running a knife around the edge. Turn out onto serving dishes. Garnish with fresh or puréed fruit, if desired.

makes 4–6 servings
preparation time: 10 minutes
cooking time: 5 minutes
chilling time: 2 hours

VARIATIONS: For extra flavor, add one of the following: 1 tsp. (5 mL) almond extract; 1 tbsp. (15 mL) concentrated fruit juice; 2 tsp. (10 mL) grated lemon or orange peel; 1 tbsp. (15 mL) of your favorite liqueur.

PER SERVING: 47 calories, 3 g protein, 6 g carbohydrate, 1 g total fat (< .5 g sat fat, < .5 g mono fat, 1 g poly fat), 1 g dietary fiber, 2 RE vitamin A, 1 mcg folate, 3 mg calcium, < .5 mg iron, 103 mg potassium, 10 mg sodium

monmouth pudding
non-dairy

VICTORIAN ENGLAND is noted for its many different puddings. This one, which was recommended for delicate stomachs, is mild tasting and easy to digest. I have replaced the milk with soy milk and reduced the sugar, butter, and jam.

4	egg whites	4
2 cups	white bread crumbs	500 mL
1 cup	vanilla soy milk, scalded	250 mL
¼ cup	sugar	60 mL
2 tbsp.	butter	30 mL
¼ cup	strawberry jam	60 mL

- Preheat oven to 325° F (165° C). Grease a 9-inch (23 cm) square baking dish.
- Beat egg whites until soft peaks form. Set aside.
- Put bread crumbs in a medium bowl. Pour scalded soy milk over them. Let soak 5 minutes, then mix in sugar and butter. Fold in beaten egg whites. Spread half the jam over bottom of baking dish. Pour half of bread crumb mixture over the jam. Layer with remaining jam and bread crumb mixture.
- Bake 30 to 40 minutes. Serve warm, plain, or with your favorite topping.
- Cold leftover pudding can be cut into squares.

makes 4 to 6 servings
preparation time: 15 minutes
baking time: 30–40 minutes

PER SERVING: 147 calories, 5 g protein, 21 g carbohydrate, 5 g total fat (3 g sat fat, 1 g mono fat, 1 g poly fat), 11 mg cholesterol, 1 g dietary fiber, 37 RE vitamin A, 14 mcg folate, 22 mg calcium, 1 mg iron, 110 mg potassium, 141 mg sodium

summer pudding

non-dairy

THIS ENGLISH pudding is one of my very favorite desserts. I enjoy it all year round but it is best when made with freshly picked ripe fruit. I have used textured soy protein as a thickener.

1 1/2 lbs.	mixed soft fruit, such as berries, chopped peaches, and apricots	675 g
1 tbsp.	lemon juice	15 mL
1 tbsp.	TSP (textured soy protein)	15 mL
1/3–1/2 cup	sugar, depending on tartness of fruit	75–125 mL
1/4 cup	soy milk	60 mL
6–8	thin slices of white bread	6–8

- In medium pot, over medium heat, bring fruit, lemon juice, TSP, sugar, and soy milk to a boil. Reduce heat to low and simmer until fruit is just soft, 3 to 5 minutes. Remove from heat.
- Grease a 9 x 5-inch (23 x 13 cm) loaf pan. Trim crusts from bread and arrange slices to cover bottom and sides of pan, reserving 2 slices. Pour fruit into bread-lined pan. Cover with remaining bread slices. Cover with foil and place a heavy weight on pudding.★
- Cool to room temperature, then chill for 24 hours.
- Just before serving, loosen pudding by running a knife around the edges; turn onto a serving platter. Cut into thick slices and, with a wide spatula, transfer to plates. Top with Best Whipped Topping (page 170) or ice cream.

makes 4 to 6 servings
preparation time: 30 minutes
chilling time: 24 hours

PER SERVING: 195 calories, 4 g protein, 43 g carbohydrate, 2 g total fat (< .5 g sat fat, < .5 g mono fat, < .5 g poly fat), 2 g dietary fiber, 172 RE vitamin A, 6 mcg folate, 60 mg vitamin C, 88 mg calcium, 2 mg iron, 147 mg potassium, 152 mg sodium

*I cut a piece of cardboard to fit snugly inside the pan and place a large paper weight in the center of it.

fruit flummery
non-dairy

TIRED OF always having the same thing for breakfast? For an unusual alternative try a fruit flummery, a popular English pudding dating back to medieval times that consists of cooked fruit, cream, and a thickening agent. In this updated version I've used plums, replaced the traditional cream with soy milk, and used cream of wheat as the thickening agent.

½ cup	water	125 mL
1 lb.	Italian plums, quartered	500 g
¾ cup	granulated sugar	175 mL
1 tbsp.	fresh lemon juice	15 mL
1 cup	soy milk	250 mL
½ cup	cream of wheat	125 mL

- Pour water into a medium pot. Add quartered plums and sugar. Bring to a boil, then reduce heat and simmer, uncovered, about 10 minutes, or until fruit is tender. Stir in lemon juice. Remove from heat.
- In a medium pot, bring soy milk and cream of wheat to a boil, stirring constantly. When mixture is a thick smooth paste, reduce heat to medium and stir in liquid from the plums. Remove from heat. Fold in plums. Spoon into cereal bowls. Serve warm or cold.

makes 4–6 servings
preparation time: 20 minutes
cooking time: 15 minutes

VARIATIONS: Instead of plums, try peaches, apricots, or gooseberries. You may need to adjust sugar content.

PER SERVING: 251 calories, 4 g protein, 58 g carbohydrate, 2 g total fat (< .5 g sat fat, < .5 g mono fat, 1 poly fat), 1 g dietary fiber, 2 RE vitamin A, 22 mcg folate, 14 mg vitamin C, 45 mg calcium, 6 mg iron, 168 mg potassium, 88 mg sodium

steamed cranberry pudding
non-dairy

DON'T SHY away from making steamed puddings; although the steaming takes a long time, the actual preparation is very quick. This moist and lightly sweetened pudding makes a wonderful dessert during the holiday season and is a nice alternative to a more traditional dairy-based pudding.

1¼ cups	unbleached flour	310 mL
¼ cup	soy flour	60 mL
1½ tsp.	baking powder	7 mL
¼ tsp.	salt	1 mL
½ tsp.	ground cinnamon	2 mL
¼ tsp.	ground ginger	1 mL
¼ tsp.	ground cloves	1 mL
¼ cup	soft or medium tofu	60 mL
⅓ cup	packed brown sugar	75 mL
1 tbsp.	soybean oil	15 mL
1	large egg	1
½ cup	vanilla soy milk	125 mL
1½ cups	chopped fresh cranberries	375 mL
¼–½ cup	raisins	60 mL–125 mL
2 tbsp.	coarsely chopped soynuts	30 mL

- Lightly grease a 6-cup (1.5L) pudding mold.
- In a medium bowl, combine flours, baking powder, salt, cinnamon, ginger, and cloves.
- In a large bowl, using an electric mixer or hand blender, beat tofu, sugar, oil, egg, and soy milk until smooth. Gradually beat in flour mixture, then fold in cranberries, raisins, and soynuts.
- Pour batter into mold. Cover tightly with foil and secure with string or a rubber band. Place mold on a rack in a large pot; add enough hot water to come halfway up sides of mold. Cover and simmer over low heat for 2½ hours, adding water as needed. Cool on wire rack for 10 minutes.★ Invert mold onto a serving platter. Slice pudding and serve with your favorite topping, such as Best Whipped Topping, page 170 or Caramel Sauce, page 172.

makes 10 servings
preparation time: 20 minutes
steaming time: 2¹/₂ hours

* Can be made up to 3 days ahead, then chilled and reheated in boiling water or microwave oven.

PER SERVING: 147 calories, 6 g protein, 25 g carbohydrate, 3 g total fat (< .5 g sat fat, < .5 g mono fat, < .5 g poly fat), 21 mg cholesterol, 3 g dietary fiber, 12 RE vitamin A, 19 mcg folate, 2 mg vitamin C, 21 mg calcium, 2 mg iron, 106 mg potassium, 139 mg sodium

persimmon pudding

I USED to walk right past persimmons in the produce section of the supermarket (where you can usually find them from October through December), oblivious to the delicate sweet taste and creamy texture of these orangy red fruits. But I was won over after I read an article singing the praises of this fruit, which though not so well known in North America, has had a long-standing following in Asian countries for centuries. The following recipe is an adaptation of Eva Powell's prizewinning persimmon pudding. She is from Mitchell, Indiana, and has won her town's annual persimmon pudding contest five times.

pulp from 4–5	ripe hachiya persimmons	(approximately 2 cups/500 mL)
1½ cups	sugar	375 mL
1	egg	1
1	egg white	1
¾ cup	buttermilk	175 mL
1 tsp.	baking soda	5 mL
1¼ cups	unbleached flour	310 mL
¼ cup	soy flour	60 mL
1 tsp.	baking powder	5 mL
½ tsp.	ground cinnamon	2 mL
	pinch of salt	
¾ cup	soy milk	175 mL
2 tbsp.	butter, melted	30 mL

- Preheat oven to 350° F (180° C). Grease a 9 x 13-inch (23 x 33 cm) baking dish.
- In large bowl, combine persimmon pulp, sugar, egg, and egg white. Mix in buttermilk and baking soda.
- Sift together flours, baking powder, cinnamon, and salt. Gradually stir into pulp mixture. Add soy milk and melted butter and stir until smooth.
- Pour batter into baking dish. Bake 55 to 60 minutes or until pudding is dark brown and a toothpick inserted in center comes out clean. Cool to room temperature, then cut into squares. Serve with Best Whipped Topping, page 170, if desired.

makes 15 servings
preparation time: 30 minutes
baking time: 55–60 minutes
freezes well

PER SERVING: 152 calories, 3 g protein, 31 g carbohydrate, 2 g total fat (1 g sat fat, 1 g mono fat, < .5 g poly fat), 17 mg cholesterol, 1 g dietary fiber, 20 RE vitamin A, 2 mcg folate, 4 mg vitamin C, 5 mg calcium, 1 mg iron, 46 mg potassium, 134 mg sodium

carrot christmas pudding

non-dairy, 1-bowl recipe

MY EARLIER book, *Tofu Mania*, includes a delicious recipe for carrot cake that many tell me is one of their favorite recipes in that book. I have adapted this delicious carrot Christmas pudding, developed years ago by our wonderful family friend Elizabeth Jones who, now in her nineties, still makes it every Christmas for her family. Always health conscious, she was excited about the addition of soy to her recipe.

¼ cup	butter or margarine, softened	60 mL
1 cup	granulated sugar	250 mL
1	egg, beaten	1
¼ cup	soft tofu	60 mL
¾ cup	unbleached flour	175 mL
¼ cup	soy flour	60 mL
½ cup each	currants and raisins	125 mL
¼ cup	grated extra firm tofu	60 mL
1 cup	grated raw potatoes	250 mL
1 cup	grated raw carrots	250 mL
¼ cup	toasted soy flakes	60 mL
1½ tsp.	baking soda	7 mL
1 tsp.	ground cinnamon	5 mL
½ tsp.	ground cloves	2 mL
1 tsp.	grated lemon or orange rind	5 mL

- Grease a 6-cup (1.5 L) pudding mold.
- In a large bowl, using an electric mixer or hand blender, beat together butter, sugar, egg, and soft tofu. Gradually mix in remaining ingredients until evenly distributed. Spoon into prepared mold. Cover tightly with foil and secure with string or a rubber band.
- Place mold on a rack in a large pot; add enough hot water to come halfway up sides of mold. Cover and simmer over low heat for 2½ to 3 hours, adding water as needed. Cool on wire rack for 10 minutes.★ Invert mold onto a serving platter. Slice pudding and serve with your favorite topping, such as Best Whipped Topping, page 170, or Lemon Sauce, page 97.

makes 10 servings
preparation time: 30 minutes
cooking time: 2¹/₂–3 hours
freezes well

*Can be made up to 3 days ahead, then chilled and reheated in boiling water or microwave oven.

PER SERVING: 265 calories, 7 g protein, 45 g carbohydrate, 7 g total fat (3 g sat fat, 2 g mono fat, < .5 g poly fat), 31 mg cholesterol, 3 g dietary fiber, 363 RE vitamin A, 39 mcg folate, 5 mg vitamin C, 26 mg calcium, 2 mg iron, 275 mg potassium, 209 mg sodium

caramel apple bread pudding
non-dairy

HUMBLE BREAD pudding takes on a new twist baked in soy milk and topped with sweet caramelized apples. Delicious.

6–8	slices leftover bread, cubed	6–8
¹⁄₃ cup	raisins	75 mL
1	medium apple, peeled, cored, and chopped	1
3	eggs	3
1–2 tbsp.	sugar	15–30 mL
2¹⁄₂ cups	vanilla soy milk	625 mL
2–3 tbsp.	Caramel Sauce, page 172	30–45 mL

- Arrange half the bread cubes in a lightly greased 8-cup (2.5 L) baking dish. Sprinkle half the raisins over bread. Repeat with remaining bread and raisins. Spread chopped apple evenly over top.
- In a medium bowl, whisk together eggs, sugar, and soy milk. Gently pour mixture over bread and apples, making sure all the bread is soaked. Cover and chill 1 hour to overnight.
- Preheat oven to 350° F (180° C). Bake pudding for 40 minutes. Remove from oven. Spoon caramel sauce over apples; return to oven and continue baking for 20 minutes or until pudding is puffy and apples are browned. Serve warm with Basic Vanilla Sauce, page 171.
- Leftover bread pudding is delicious cold or warmed up in the microwave oven.

**makes 6–8 servings
preparation time: pudding, 15 minutes;
caramel sauce, 10 minutes
baking time: 60 minutes**

PER SERVING: 157 calories, 6 g protein, 25 g carbohydrate, 4 g total fat (1 g sat fat, 1 g mono fat, 1 g poly fat), 70 mg cholesterol, 2 g dietary fiber, 35 RE vitamin A, 36 mcg folate, 2 vitamin C, 78 g calcium, 2 mg iron, 212 mg potassium, 147 mg sodium

custards, mousses, souffles & trifles

banana apple cranberry custard flan

non-dairy

THIS DELICIOUSLY healthy dessert is a favorite in my home. I've replaced all the cream with soy milk and scratched two eggs from the original recipe. The three fruits complement each other and the resulting flavors and creamy texture are irresistible.

2	large apples, peeled, cored, and thinly sliced	2
1 cup	cranberries, fresh or frozen	250 mL
1	banana, sliced	1
¼ cup	granulated sugar	60 mL
2 tsp.	grated orange peel	10 mL
1	egg	1
1 cup	vanilla soy milk	250 mL
1 tbsp.	soy flour	15 mL
2 tbsp.	concentrated orange juice	30 mL
1 tbsp.	brown sugar	15 mL

- Preheat oven to 375° F (190° C). Grease a 9-inch (23 cm) square shallow baking dish.
- In a large bowl, combine apples, cranberries, banana, granulated sugar, and orange peel. Spread over bottom of baking dish.
- In a small bowl, beat together egg, soy milk, flour, and orange juice. Pour evenly over fruit. Sprinkle with brown sugar.
- Bake 30 to 40 minutes, or until puffed and golden. Cool to room temperature. Serve plain, with ice cream or Caramel Sauce (page 172) drizzled over it.

makes 5 to 6 servings
preparation time: 20 minutes
baking time: 30–40 minutes

VARIATIONS: try other combinations of fruit and berries

PER SERVING: 124 calories, 3 g protein, 25 g carbohydrate, 2 g total fat (< .5 g sat fat, < .5 g mono fat, 1 g poly fat), 31 mg cholesterol, 3 g dietary fiber, 21 RE vitamin A, 11 mcg folate, 9 mg vitamin C, 14 mg calcium, 1 mg iron, 226 mg potassium, 16 mg sodium

ENJOY THE same frothy light texture and rich flavor that the traditional Italian dessert is noted for, without all the saturated fat and cholesterol.

2 tbsp.	granulated sugar, or to taste	30 mL
1 cup	vanilla soy milk	250 mL
½ cup	liquid egg substitute	125 mL
¼ cup	dry Marsala wine	60 mL

- Combine sugar and soy milk in a medium saucepan. Bring to a boil over medium heat, whisking constantly. Remove from heat. Stir a small amount of the soy milk mixture into the egg substitute, then pour this back into saucepan. Whisk vigorously over low heat until almost bubbly. Do not boil. Whisk in Marsala wine. Remove from heat. Zabaglione should be light and frothy.
- Pour into wine glasses and serve immediately.

makes about 2 cups (500 mL), or 4–5 servings
preparation time: 15 minutes

PER SERVING: 58 calories, 3 g protein, 7 g carbohydrate, 1 g total fat (< .5 g sat fat, < .5 g mono fat, < .5 g poly fat), 1 g dietary fiber, 1 RE vitamin A, 1 mcg folate, 2 mg calcium, < .5 mg Iron, 70 mg potassium, 42 mg sodium

crème caramel à l'orange

non-dairy

I LOVE Crème Caramel so much that I'm including it here even though there's also a recipe for it in *Tofu Mania*. In that version I replaced the cream called for in the original recipe with tofu. This time, I've used soy milk and I am thrilled with the results. This custard has a wonderfully smooth texture and lovely taste.

⅓ cup	sugar (to caramelize pudding mold)	75 mL
3 tbsp.	water	45 mL
2 cups	vanilla soy milk	500 mL
3	large eggs	3
¼ cup	sugar	60 mL
2 tbsp.	Grand Marnier or other liqueur	30 mL

- Preheat oven to 325° F (165° C). Combine ⅓ cup (75 mL) sugar and water in a small heavy stainless steel saucepan. Over medium-high heat, stir until sugar has completely dissolved and turned golden. Immediately pour it into an ovenproof 5-cup (1.25 L) pudding mold and tilt the mold so that the caramel will coat the sides. Set aside.
- Scald the soy milk.
- In a medium bowl, using a whisk, blend together eggs, sugar, and Grand Marnier. Whisk in soy milk. Pour mixture into caramelized mold and set in a pan of hot water. Poach in oven for 1 hour, 15 minutes. Do not overcook as this will cause the custard to be lumpy. Remove from oven. Cool to room temperature, then chill at least 3 hours or overnight.
- To unmold, run a knife around the edge of the custard, then loosen it by gently moving the mold back and forth in a circular fashion. Place a serving platter over the mold, then invert to unmold.

**makes 4–6 servings
preparation time: 15 minutes
baking time: 1 hour, 15 minutes
chilling time: 3 hours to overnight**

PER SERVING: 150 calories, 5 g protein, 21 g carbohydrate, 4 g total fat (1 g sat fat, 1 g mono fat, 1 g poly fat), 94 mg cholesterol, 1 g dietary fiber, 44 RE vitamin A, 12 mcg folate, 14 mg calcium, 1 mg iron, 144 mg potassium, 38 mg sodium

irish coffee crème caramel

CUSTARDS DON'T get any better than this—wonderful flavor, extra smooth texture, and thanks to the substitution of soy milk for cow's milk, just 1.5 grams of saturated fat per serving!

⅓ cup	sugar (to caramelize mold)	75 mL
3 tbsp.	water	45 mL
2 cups	vanilla soy milk	500 mL
1 tbsp.	instant coffee granules	15 mL
3	large eggs	3
¼ cup	sugar	60 mL
2 tbsp.	Irish Cream	30 mL

- Proceed as for Crème Caramel à l'Orange, page 158, except, add the coffee granules to the hot soy milk and substitute Irish Cream for the Grand Marnier.

makes 4–6 servings
preparation time: 10 minutes
baking time: 1 hour, 15 minutes
chilling time: 3 hours to overnight

PER SERVING: 162 calories, 6 g protein, 23 g carbohydrate, 5 g total fat (1 g sat fat, 1 g mono fat, 1 g poly fat), 107 mg cholesterol, 1 g dietary fiber, 52 RE vitamin A, 13 mcg folate, 17 mg calcium, 1 mg iron, 150 mg potassium, 46 mg sodium

coffee tortoni

AN ELEGANT rich-tasting dessert for coffee and ice cream lovers, which makes it a good dessert to have on hand for unexpected guests.

3	egg whites	3
¾ cup	granulated sugar	175 mL
½ cup	soft tofu	125 mL
1 tbsp.	instant coffee granules	15 mL
2 tsp.	rum	10 mL
1 cup	whipping cream	250 mL
1–2 tbsp.	honey-roasted soynuts	15–30 mL
	chocolate-covered espresso beans, as a garnish (optional)	

- In a large bowl, beat egg whites until soft peaks form. Gradually beat in sugar until whites are stiff.
- In a small bowl, with electric hand blender, blend together tofu, coffee granules, and rum. Blend into egg whites.
- In a medium bowl, whip cream. Fold cream into egg white mixture. Stir in 1 tbsp. (15 mL) crushed soynuts. Spoon into parfait glasses; cover and freeze until ready to serve. Sprinkle with remaining crushed soynuts and garnish with chocolate-covered espresso beans, if desired. Let stand 5 to 10 minutes at room temperature before serving.

makes 6–8 servings
preparation time: 15 minutes
freezing time: at least 3 hours

PER SERVING: 195 calories, 3 g protein, 20 g carbohydrate, 12 g total fat (7 g sat fat, 3 g mono fat, < .5 g poly fat), 41 mg cholesterol, < .5 g dietary fiber, 127 RE vitamin A, 1 mcg folate, < .5 mg vitamin C, 26 mg calcium, < .5 mg iron, 84 mg potassium, 34 mg sodium

chocolate pots de crème

non-dairy

CHOCOLATE LOVERS, are you ready? Here's a creamy smooth chocolatey treat you're sure to love. I've replaced a portion of the chocolate with soy milk powder, but you'd never know.

4 oz.	semi-sweet chocolate, chopped	125 g
½ cup	hot vanilla soy milk	125 mL
2 tbsp.	soy milk powder	30 mL
1	egg	1
1	egg white	1
1–2 tbsp.	Tia Maria or other liqueur	15–30 mL
	Best Whipped Topping, as a garnish, page 170 (optional)	

- Place chopped chocolate in a medium bowl. Pour hot soy milk over chocolate and stir until completely melted. Stir in soy milk powder.
- In a small bowl, whisk together egg and egg white; then whisk into chocolate mixture. Add Tia Maria.
- Pour into 6 2-oz. (60 mL) pots de crème or demitasse cups. Cover and chill until set. Garnish with Best Whipped Topping, if desired.

makes 6 servings
preparation time: 10 minutes

PER SERVING: 133 calories, 4 g protein, 13 g carbohydrate, 7 g total fat ($<$.5 g sat fat, $<$.5 g mono fat, $<$.5 g poly fat), 31 mg cholesterol, 1 g dietary fiber, 15 RE vitamin A, 14 mcg folate, 11 mg calcium, $<$.5 mg iron, 110 mg potassium, 22 mg sodium

custards, mousses, souffles & trifles

chocolate mousse
non-dairy

A MUST for chocolate lovers, this airy mousse is easy to prepare. I also like to freeze it in parfait glasses, which makes for an exceptionally smooth and creamy texture.

½ cup	hot soy milk	125 mL
¼ cup	hot strong coffee	60 mL
8 oz.	semi-sweet chocolate, chopped	225 mL
2 tbsp.	orange brandy	30 mL
4	eggs, separated	4
1	egg white	1

- Combine soy milk and coffee in a medium bowl. Stir in chocolate until completely melted. Stir in brandy and egg yolks, one at a time.
- In a large bowl, beat all 5 egg whites until stiff. Gradually pour chocolate mixture into egg whites and blend until just combined.
- Pour mousse into individual serving bowls or parfait glasses. Cover and chill at least 3 hours or overnight.

makes 8–9 servings
preparation time: 15 minutes

VARIATIONS: Freeze mousse and serve as ice cream. Very smooth and creamy!

PER SERVING: 167 calories, 4 g protein, 14 g carbohydrate, 9 g total fat (1 g sat fat, 1 g mono fat, < .5 g poly fat), 83 mg cholesterol, < .5 g dietary fiber, 38 RE vitamin A, 10 mcg folate, 10 mg calcium, < .5 mg iron, 53 mg potassium, 32 mg sodium

AN IRRESISTIBLE combination of tropical fruits, soy yogurt, and whipped light cream.

3 cups	chopped tropical fruit mix (pineapple, kiwi, mango, peach, cantaloupe), fresh or frozen	750 mL
⅓ cup	cold water	75 mL
2 tbsp.	(2 pkgs.) unflavored gelatin	14 g
½ cup	granulated sugar	125 mL
2 tbsp.	lemon juice	30 mL
2 tbsp.	rum	30 mL
1 cup	vanilla soy yogurt	250 mL
1 cup	whipping cream	250 mL
1	egg white	1
	toasted shredded coconut, as a garnish (optional)	

- In a food processor, purée fruit (can be left a little chunky, if desired).
- Pour water into a small saucepan and sprinkle gelatin over it. Heat over low heat just until gelatin is dissolved.
- Meanwhile, in a large bowl, combine puréed fruit, sugar, lemon juice, rum, yogurt, and dissolved gelatin.
- In a separate bowl, whip cream.
- In a small bowl, beat egg white until stiff.
- Fold whipped cream and beaten egg white into fruit mixture. Spoon mousse into individual dessert bowls. Cover and chill 4 hours to overnight. Just before serving, garnish with coconut, if desired.

makes 8–10 servings
preparation time: 30 minutes
chilling time: 4 hours to overnight

PER SERVING: 180 calories, 3 g protein, 21 g carbohydrate, 9 g total fat (5 g sat fat, 3 g mono fat, < .5 poly fat), 33 mg cholesterol, 1 g dietary fiber, 190 RE vitamin A, 1 mcg folate, 45 mg vitamin C, 19 mg calcium, < .5 mg iron, 27 mg potassium, 23 mg sodium

zesty lime mousse

THIS REFRESHING mousse is easy to make and can be prepared a day ahead.

½ cup	fresh lime juice	125 mL
½ cup	sugar	125 mL
1 tbsp.	(1 pkg.) unflavored gelatin	15 mL
1 cup	soy milk	250 mL
2 tsp.	grated lime peel	10 mL
1 cup	whipping cream	250 mL
1	lime, thinly sliced, as a garnish	1
	caramelized sugar (below) as a garnish (optional)	

- In a small saucepan, combine lime juice with sugar. Sprinkle with gelatin. Heat over low, stirring until gelatin and sugar have dissolved.
- Pour soy milk into a medium bowl. Stir in gelatin mixture and lime peel.
- In a separate bowl, whip cream, then blend into lime and soy milk mixture. Spoon into parfait glasses. Cover and chill until set, 4 hours to overnight. To serve, garnish with slices of lime and/or caramelized sugar.
- *To caramelize sugar*, pour 3 tbsp. (45 mL) sugar into a small saucepan and heat over medium-high heat, stirring constantly, until sugar has melted and turned golden in color. Remove from heat. Continue to stir for 1 minute until caramelized sugar thickens slightly. Coat a spoon with it and let the sugar drizzle over the mousse in a circular or zigzag fashion. Serve within 1 hour while the caramelized sugar is still crunchy.

makes 8–10 servings
preparation and cooking time: mousse, 15 minutes;
caramelized sugar, 10 minutes

VARIATIONS: For Key Lime pie, pour mousse into a graham cracker crumb crust and chill.

PER SERVING: 210 calories, 3 g protein, 22 g carbohydrate, 13 g total fat (8 g sat fat, 4 g mono fat, 1 g poly fat), 44 mg cholesterol, 1 g dietary fiber, 119 RE vitamin A, 5 mcg folate, 10 mg vitamin C, 36 mg calcium, < .5 mg iron, 132 mg potassium, 21 mg sodium

lemon custard soufflé

THIS TASTY combination of spongy soufflé on the top and creamy custard on the bottom makes for a delicious light dessert.

¹⁄₄ cup	butter or margarine, at room temperature	60 mL
¹⁄₂ cup	sugar, divided	125 mL
3	eggs, separated	3
1 tbsp.	grated lemon peel	15 mL
¹⁄₄ cup	unbleached flour	60 mL
1 tbsp.	soy flour	15 mL
1 cup	vanilla soy milk	250 mL
¹⁄₃ cup	fresh lemon juice	75 mL

- Preheat oven to 350° F (180° C). Grease a 7 x 7 x 3½-inch (18 x 18 x 9 cm) casserole dish.
- In a medium bowl, combine butter with half the sugar until smooth. Mix in egg yolks and lemon peel, then stir in flours, soy milk, and lemon juice until smooth.
- In a separate bowl, beat egg whites until frothy; add remaining sugar and beat until stiff. Fold into flour mixture. Pour into greased dish and set in a pan of hot water. Poach in oven for 40 to 45 minutes, or until top is lightly browned. Serve warm or at room temperature.

makes 5–to 6 servings
preparation time: 20 minutes
baking time: 40–45 minutes

PER SERVING: 204 calories, 5 g protein, 23 g carbohydrate, 11 g total fat (6 g sat fat, 3 g mono fat, 1 g poly fat), 114 mg cholesterol, 1 g dietary fiber, 115 RE vitamin A, 13 mcg folate, 8 mg vitamin C, 17 mg calcium, 1 mg iron, 106 mg potassium, 35 mg sodium

chocolate orange soufflé
non-dairy

BEAUTIFUL TO look at and even better to eat, this soufflé makes a special occasion dessert. I've replaced the butter called for in the original recipe with soy milk.

1 oz.	semi-sweet chocolate, chopped	28 g
2 tbsp.	vanilla soy milk	30 mL
2 tsp.	grated orange peel	10 mL
2	eggs, separated	2
2 tbsp.	granulated sugar, divided	30 mL
	pinch of cream of tartar	

- Butter 3 individual 3-inch (10 cm) ramekins. Also butter three 3-inch (10 cm) wide strips of aluminum foil and wrap around each ramekin, buttered side in, securing them with string or tape.
- Preheat oven to 375° F (190° C).
- In a small bowl, microwave chocolate and soy milk until hot. Remove from microwave oven and stir to melt chocolate; stir in orange peel.
- In a medium bowl, whisk together egg yolks and 1 tbsp. (15 mL) sugar. Whisk in chocolate mixture.
- In a separate bowl, beat egg whites with cream of tartar until soft peaks form. Add remaining 1 tbsp. (15 mL) sugar and beat until stiff. Gradually fold egg whites into chocolate mixture. Fill ramekins. Place ramekins on baking sheet.
- Bake 18 to 20 minutes, or until well puffed. Remove string and foil. Serve immediately before soufflé deflates.

makes 3 servings (recipe can easily be doubled)
preparation time: 20 minutes
baking time: 18–20 minutes

PER SERVING: 127 calories, 4 g protein, 14 g carbohydrate, 6 g total fat (1 g sat fat, 1 g mono fat, < .5 g poly fat), 125 mg cholesterol, < .5 g dietary fiber, 57 RE vitamin A, 14 mcg folate, 2 mg vitamin C, 17 mg calcium, 1 mg iron, 53 mg potassium, 38 mg sodium

A BEAUTIFUL classic dessert for a festive occasion.

2½ cups	Orange Brandy Custard Sauce, page 168	625 mL
1	pound cake (See Almond Pound Cake, page 122)	8 x 4-inch
4 tbsp.	orange brandy	60 mL
4 tbsp.	water	60 mL
1 cup	raspberry jam, warmed	250 mL
1	large or 2 medium seedless oranges, peeled and sliced crosswise into thin rounds	1
2 cups	fresh raspberries	500 mL
¾ cup	whipping cream	175 mL
1–2 tbsp.	sugar	15–30 mL
½ cup	soft tofu, puréed	125 mL
½ tsp.	vanilla extract	2 mL
1 tbsp.	toasted soy flakes or sliced almonds, optional	15 mL

- Make Orange Brandy Custard Sauce. Set aside to cool.
- Cut cake into 2-inch (5 cm) cubes. Spread half the cubes over the bottom of a large glass bowl. Combine the brandy and water and sprinkle cake with half the mixture; drizzle with half the jam; layer with half the orange slices and half the berries; top with half the custard sauce. Repeat layering, ending with the custard sauce. Cover and refrigerate at least 4 hours or overnight.
- Shortly before serving, using a medium bowl, whip cream with sugar until stiff. Blend puréed tofu and vanilla into whipped cream. Garnish trifle with dollops of cream and sprinkle with toasted sliced almonds or soy flakes, if desired.

makes 10–12 servings
preparation time:20 minutes to assemble trifle
 and make cream topping (does not include making cake and custard)

PER SERVING: 296 calories, 6 g protein, 52 g carbohydrate, 9 g total fat (4 g sat fat, 2 g mono fat, 1 g poly fat), 38 mg cholesterol, 2 g dietary fiber, 85 RE vitamin A, 20 mcg folate, 11 mg vitamin C, 36 mg calcium, 1 mg iron, 148 mg potassium, 108 mg sodium

orange brandy custard sauce

⅓ cup	granulated sugar	75 mL
1 tbsp.	cornstarch	15 mL
½ cup	vanilla soy milk	375 mL
1	egg yolk	1
1 tbsp.	concentrated orange juice	15 mL
1–2 tbsp.	orange brandy	15–30 mL

- In a medium saucepan, combine sugar and cornstarch. Stir in 2 tbsp (30mL) of the soy milk until smooth. Gradually whisk in rest of soy milk. Cook and continue to whisk over medium heat until thickened and bubbly. Remove from heat.
- In a small bowl, stir a spoonful of the hot mixture into the egg yolk. Pour back into saucepan. Cook and stir over low heat until nearly bubbly. Stir in orange juice and brandy. Remove from heat. Cover and chill until ready to serve.

makes about 2½ cups (625mL)
prepration time 10 minutes

PER TBSP (ORANGE BRANDY CUSTARD SAUCE): 13.35 calories, .32 g protein, 2.15 g carbohydrate, .30 g total fat (.06 g sat fat, .08 g mono fat, .09 g poly fat), 5.19 mg cholesterol, .12 g dietary fiber, 2.75 RE vitamin A, 1.40 mcg folate, .60 mg vitamine C, 1.08 mg calcium, .07 mg iron, 16.20 mg potassium, 1.30 mg sodium

creams & sauces

best whipped topping

DO YOU love the taste of freshly whipped cream but wish it didn't have to be so fatty? This all-natural light and velvety topping is the ultimate cream fantasy—without all the calories. Garnish pies, cakes, and puddings with this versatile topping or use it as a dip for fresh fruit.

½ cup	whipping cream	125 mL
2 tbsp.	granulated sugar	30 mL
1	egg white	1
⅓ cup	soft tofu	75 mL
½ tsp.	vanilla extract	2 mL
1 tbsp.	crushed honey-roasted soynuts (optional)	15 mL

- In a medium bowl, whip cream with sugar.
- In a small bowl, beat egg white until stiff. In a separate bowl, using the same beaters, beat tofu with vanilla. Blend egg white and tofu mixture into whipped cream. Fold in crushed soynuts, if desired.

makes about 1 cup
preparation time: 10 minutes

VARIATIONS: 1) To make parfaits, freeze topping in individual bowls. Let stand 5–10 minutes at room temperature before serving.
2) For other flavorings, use liqueurs, fruit concentrates, and other extracts instead of vanilla.

PER TBSP (15 mL): 24 calories, < .5 g protein, 1 g carbohydrate, 2 g total fat (1 g sat fat, 1 g mono fat, < .5 g poly fat), 7 mg cholesterol, < .5 mg dietary fiber, 21 RE vitamin A, < .5 mcg folate, < .5 mg vitamin C, 4 mg calcium, < .5 mg iron, 13 mg potassium, 4 mg sodium

USE THIS quick and easy sauce as a topping for cakes, puddings, and fresh fruit.

3 tbsp.	sugar	45 mL
¼ cup	cornstarch	60 mL
2½ cups	vanilla soy milk	625 mL
1	egg yolk	1

- In a medium saucepan, combine sugar and cornstarch. Whisk in soy milk and egg yolk. Over medium heat, whisking constantly, cook mixture until sauce is thickened and smooth. Remove from heat. Cover surface of sauce with plastic wrap to prevent a skin from forming. Serve warm or cold.

makes just under 3 cups (750 ml)
preparation time: 5 minutes
cooking time: about 5 minutes

PER TBSP (15 mL): 11 calories, < .5 g protein, 2 g carbohydrate, < .5 g total fat (< .5 g sat fat, < .5 g mono fat, < .5 g poly fat), 40 mg cholesterol, < .5 g dietary fiber, 2 RE vitamin A, 1 mcg folate, 1 mg calcium, < .5 mg iron, 18 mg potassium, 2 mg sodium

caramel sauce

non-dairy, 1-bowl recipe

AN EXTRA boost of soy in the form of creamy soy milk replaces the water used in more traditional recipes. Almost fat-free, this delicious sauce is a great topping for puddings, cakes, and ice cream.

1 cup	packed brown sugar	250 mL
1 tsp.	ground cinnamon	5 mL
½ cup	soy milk	125 mL
¼ cup	corn syrup	60 mL

- In a medium saucepan, combine all ingredients. Over medium heat, stirring occasionally, bring mixture to a boil. Reduce heat to low and simmer uncovered about 5 minutes. Serve warm or cold.

makes 1¾ cups (425 ml)
preparation and cooking time: 10 minutes
keeps in refrigerator for up to one week and freezes well

PER TBSP (15 mL): 55 calories, < .5 g protein, 14 g carbohydrate, < .5 g total fat (< .5 g sat fat, < .5 g mono fat, < .5 g poly fat), < .5 g dietary fiber, < .5 RE vitamin A, < .5 mcg folate, < .5 mg vitamin C, 11 mg calcium, < .5 mg iron, 47 mg potassium, 10 mg sodium

chocolate **soynut butter** sauce

A RICH-tasting chocolately sauce, ideal as a topping for ice cream and puddings or as a dipping sauce for fresh fruit and sliced cake.

¾ cup	vanilla soy milk	175 mL
¼ cup	corn syrup	60 mL
2 oz.	semi-sweet chocolate, chopped	56 g
1 tbsp.	soynut butter	15 mL
1 tbsp.	butter	15 mL

• In a medium saucepan, bring soy milk and corn syrup to a boil. Remove from heat. Stir in chocolate and soynut butter until melted; then stir in butter. Cover and chill until ready to serve. Keeps up to 1 week.

makes about 1 cup (250 ml)
preparation and cooking time: 15 minutes
freezes well

VARIATIONS: For plain chocolate sauce, substitute 1 oz. (28 g) semi-sweet chocolate for the 1 tbsp. (15 mL) soynut butter.

PER TBSP (15 mL): 48 calories, 1 g protein, 6 g carbohydrate, 2 g total fat (1 g sat fat, < .5 g mono fat, < .5 g poly fat), 2 mg cholesterol, < .5 g dietary fiber*, 7 RE vitamin A*, < .5 mcg folate*, 1 mg calcium*, < .5 mg iron*, 23 mg potassium, 13 mg sodium

lemon curd

non-dairy, 1-bowl recipe

SOY MILK replaces the butter in this all-natural, almost fat-free recipe. Add extra flavor to your favorite desserts by stirring lemon curd into cake and pie fillings or by using it as a topping.

⅔ cup	granulated sugar	150 mL
1 tbsp.	grated lemon peel	15 mL
2	eggs, beaten	2
⅔ cup	fresh lemon juice, strained	150 mL
2 tbsp.	vanilla soy milk	30 mL

- In a medium saucepan, over low heat, whisk together sugar, lemon peel, and eggs. Cook until sugar dissolves, then whisk in lemon juice and soy milk. Continue to cook over low heat, stirring constantly, until mixture thinly coats a spoon. Do not boil. Remove from heat. Curd will thicken as it cools.

makes just over 1 cup (250 ml)
preparation and cooking time: 15 minutes
freezes well

PER TBSP (15 mL): 41 calories, 1 g protein, 9 g carbohydrate, 1 g total fat (< .5 g sat fat, < .5 g mono fat, < .5 g poly fat), 22 mg cholesterol, < .5 g dietary fiber, 10 RE vitamin A, 4 mcg folate, 5 mg vitamin C, 4 mg calcium, < .5 mg iron, 21 mg potassium, 7 mg sodium

THIS DELICATELY flavored cream is a great topping for pies, cakes, and puddings.

¹⁄₂ cup	whipping cream	125 mL
2 tsp.	sugar	10 mL
1¹⁄₄ cups	(1 container) tofu almond dessert	300 g
1 tbsp.	toasted, sliced almonds (optional)	15 mL

- In a medium bowl, whip cream with sugar until stiff.
- In a small bowl, purée tofu almond dessert. Fold into whipped cream. Sprinkle with almonds, if desired.

makes about 2¹⁄₄ cups (560 ml)
preparation time: 5 minutes

PER TBSP (15 mL): 17 calories, 3 g protein, 12 g carbohydrate, 1 g total fat (1 g sat fat, < .5 g mono fat, < .5 g poly fat), 4 mg cholesterol, 14 RE vitamin A, < .5 mcg folate, < .5 mg vitamin C, 2 mg calcium, 11 mg potassium, 1 mg sodium

orange cream

GREAT AS a dip for fresh fruit or as a topping for pies and cakes.

½ cup	whipping cream	125 mL
3 tbsp.	sugar	45 mL
½ cup	soft or medium tofu	125 mL
1 tbsp.	fresh orange juice	15 mL
2 tsp.	grated orange peel	10 mL

- Whip cream and sugar in a medium bowl until stiff. Using the same beaters, purée tofu, orange juice, and peel in a small bowl. Blend into whipped cream. Serve same day.

makes approximately 1⅔ cups (400 ml)
preparation time: 10 minutes

PER TBSP (15 mL): 23 calories, < .5 g protein, 2 g carbohydrate, 2 g total fat (1 g sat fat, < .5 g mono fat, < .5 g poly fat), 6 mg cholesterol, < .5 g dietary fiber, 18 RE vitamin A, < .5 mcg folate, < .5 mg vitamin C, 5 mg calcium, < .5 mg iron, 14 mg potassium, 2 mg sodium

berries with orange ricotta cream

IS THERE a more delicious refreshing summer dessert than berries and cream? This rich tasting cream is light yet satisfying. For a non-dairy version, you can replace the ricotta cheese with an additional 6-oz. (175 mL) container of soy yogurt.

½ cup	low-fat ricotta cheese	125 mL
6 oz.	(1 container) vanilla soy or regular vanilla yogurt	175 mL
¾ cup	soft tofu	175 mL
1 tsp.	grated orange peel	5 mL
2 tbsp.	fresh orange juice	30 mL
2 tbsp.	sugar	30 mL
2 cups	mixed berries	500 mL
4 tsp.	honey roasted soynuts (optional)	20 mL

- In a medium bowl, with electric hand blender, blend first six ingredients until smooth. Cover and chill until ready to serve.
- Place berries in dessert bowls and top with cream. Sprinkle with soynuts, if desired.

makes 4 servings
preparation time: 10 minutes

PER SERVING: 152 calories, 10 g protein, 25 g carbohydrate, 3 g total fat (1 g sat fat, < .5 g mono fat, < .5 g poly fat), 5 mg cholesterol, 4 g dietary fiber, 37 RE vitamin A, 2 mcg folate, 6 mg vitamin C, 192 mg calcium, 2 mg iron, 275 mg potassium, 72 mg sodium

strawberry fool

A QUICK make-ahead dessert, this light fruit cream is a refreshing end to any meal.

1 cup	whipping cream, whipped	250 mL
1 cup	soft tofu, puréed	250 mL
4 cups	strawberries, puréed	1 L
2 tbsp.	frozen orange juice concentrate	30 mL
½ cup	granulated sugar	125 mL
2 tbsp.	honey-roasted soynuts, chopped or crushed (optional)	30 mL

- Combine whipped cream and puréed tofu. In a separate bowl, combine puréed strawberries, orange juice, and sugar. Reserve ½ cup (125 mL) of this mixture and fold the rest into the cream/tofu mixture. Pour Strawberry Fool into individual dessert bowls, cover, and refrigerate (can be made several hours ahead). Just before serving, drizzle remaining strawberry sauce over Fool. Sprinkle with soynuts, if desired.

makes 8–10 servings
preparation time: 20 minutes

VARIATIONS: Use any raw or cooked fruit such as berries or rhubarb. The sugar may need to be adjusted depending on the tartness of the fruit.

PER SERVING: 261 calories, 3 g protein, 39 g carbohydrate, 11 g total fat (6 g sat fat, 3 g mono fat, < .5 g poly fat), 33 mg cholesterol, 2 g dietary fiber, 120 RE vitamin A, 6 mcg folate, 29 mg vitamin C, 25 mg calcium, 1 mg iron, 92 mg potassium, 11 mg sodium

margarita dip with fresh fruit

IDEAL FOR a large crowd, this refreshing and luscious dessert with tropical flair will appeal to everyone.

4 cups	mixed fresh fruit (such as pineapple, cantaloupe, watermelon, mango, and kiwi) cut up into bite-sized pieces	1 L

dip

4 oz.	soy cream cheese	125 g
6 oz.	(1 container) vanilla soy yogurt	175 g
¼ cup	soft tofu	60 mL
1–2 tbsp.	tequila	15–30 mL
1 tbsp.	orange juice concentrate	15 mL
1 tbsp.	fresh lime juice	15 mL
1 tsp.	grated lime peel	5 mL
½ cup	whipping cream, whipped	125 mL

- In a blender or food processor, blend all dip ingredients except whipped cream until smooth. Fold in whipped cream. Cover and chill until ready to serve. Can be made up to 4 hours ahead.
- Just before serving, transfer dip to a glass bowl and place in the center of a large round serving platter. Arrange cut up fruit around the dip.

makes about 2 cups (500 mL) of dip
preparation time: 15 minutes

PER TBSP (15 mL): 32 calories, 1 g protein, 2 g carbohydrate, 2 g total fat (1 g sat fat, < .5 g mono fat, 1 g poly fat), 5 mg cholesterol, < .5 g dietary fiber, 18 RE vitamin A, 1 mcg folate, 1 mg vitamin C, 38 mg calcium, < .5 mg iron, 11 mg potassium, 21 mg sodium

confections

amaretto drops

A TASTY confection to add to your dessert tray during the holiday season. Or wrap them up and give them to your friends. No cooking required!

4 oz.	soy cream cheese	125 g
3 cups	confectioner's sugar	750 mL
1 tbsp.	Amaretto liqueur	15 mL
½ cup	unsweetened shredded coconut	125 mL
¼ cup	toasted soy flakes	60 mL
½ cup	dried cranberries	125 mL

- In a medium bowl, using a fork, combine cream cheese, sugar, and Amaretto until fluffy. Gradually stir in remaining ingredients. Using 2 teaspoons, shape into ¾-inch (2 cm) balls and scrape into paper candy cups.★ Cover and chill until firm, about 2 hours.

makes 40–48 drops
preparation time: 30 minutes
freezes well

*Paper candy cups are available in most supermarkets where paper muffin cups are sold.

PER DROP: 53 calories, 1 g protein, 10 g carbohydrate, 1 g total fat (< .5 g sat fat, < .5 g mono fat, 1 g poly fat), 1 g dietary fiber, 1 RE vitamin A, < .5 mcg folate, 1 mg vitamin C, 1 mg calcium, < .5 mg iron, 9 mg potassium, 14 mg sodium

chocolate caramels

non-dairy, 1-bowl recipe

HAVE THESE low-fat, soft, and chewy caramels in a candy dish when friends and family come for a visit. I have replaced all the cream called for in the original recipe with soy milk.

½ cup	sugar	125 mL
1 cup	vanilla soy milk	250 mL
1 tbsp.	butter or margarine	15 mL
1 tsp.	honey	5 mL
2 tsp.	unsweetened cocoa powder, sifted	10 mL

- Over medium heat, melt the sugar in a small saucepan, stirring until it has completely dissolved and is light golden in color. Gradually stir in soy milk and bring mixture to a boil. Reduce heat to low and let simmer 10 to 15 minutes, uncovered. Add butter, honey, and cocoa and continue boiling and stirring for another 10 to 15 minutes, or until mixture thickens and shrinks away from the bottom and side of the pan. Pour onto a greased or parchment-lined pan and let cool 10 minutes.

- While still warm, cut caramel into approximately 18 pieces. Wrap in individual candy wrappers.

makes 18 caramel candies
preparation time: 25 minutes
cooking time: 20–30 minutes
freezes well

PER CARAMEL: 34 calories, < .5 g protein, 6 g carbohydrate, 1 g total fat (< .5 g sat fat, < .5 g mono fat, < .5 g poly fat), 2 mg cholesterol, < .5 g dietary fiber, 6 RE vitamin A, < .5 mcg folate, 1 mg calcium, < .5 mg iron, 29 mg potassium, 2 mg sodium

chocolate caramel truffles

BY COMBINING soy milk with soy milk powder, I've achieved a creamy texture similar to whipping cream but without the saturated fat. These superb tasting truffles should satisfy the most discriminating chocolate lovers (you know who you are!).

²/₃ cup	vanilla soy milk	150 mL
3 tbsp.	soy milk powder	45 mL
1 cup	granulated sugar	250 mL
6 oz.	bittersweet or semi-sweet chocolate, chopped	225 g
1 tbsp.	butter, cut up	15 mL
¹/₄ cup	unsweetened cocoa powder	60 mL

- Pour soy milk into a medium microwavable bowl and microwave on high for 60 seconds, or until hot. Using an electric hand blender, blend soy milk powder into hot soy milk until mixture is smooth and creamy.

- In a medium stainless steel saucepan, heat sugar over medium high heat, stirring constantly until sugar is dissolved and pale golden in color. Remove from heat. Slowly stir hot soy milk into caramelized sugar. Continue to stir over low heat for 5 to 10 minutes, or until sugar is completely dissolved. Stir in chocolate until it is melted; then stir in butter. Transfer to a bowl, cover and let set until mixture is firm enough to shape into truffles, at least 1 hour.

- Using your hands or a melon baller, shape chocolate mixture into 1-inch (2.5 cm) balls (they can be somewhat irregular in shape) and roll in cocoa powder. Place truffles in paper cups, if desired. Cover and chill until ready to serve. Leftover truffles must be chilled to maintain firmness.

makes about 36 truffles
preparation time: 40 minutes
chilling time: 1 hour or longer
freezes well

PER TRUFFLE: 53 calories, 1 g protein, 9 g carbohydrate, 2 g total fat (1 g sat fat, 1 g mono fat, < .5 g poly fat), 1 mg cholesterol, 1 g dietary fiber, 3 RE vitamin A, 2 mcg folate, 3 mg calcium, < .5 mg iron, 32 mg potassium, 2 mg sodium

chocolate soynut butter truffles

TRADITIONAL TRUFFLES are loaded with butter and cream, whereas these fat-reduced delicate morsels get their rich flavor and creamy texture from soynut butter, honey, soy protein isolate, and, of course, chocolate! You can whip up these delicious little confections in just a few minutes.

4 oz.	semi-sweet chocolate (or 2 oz. semi-sweet + 2 oz. milk chocolate) chopped	125 g
2 tbsp.	honey	30 mL
1 tsp.	butter	5 mL
1 tsp.	soynut butter	5 mL
3–4 tbsp.	soy protein isolate	60 mL
	cocoa powder, shredded coconut, or ground nuts (optional)	

- In a medium microwavable bowl, combine chopped chocolate with honey and butter. Microwave on high for 15 seconds. Stir and microwave another 15 seconds, or until chocolate is almost completely melted. Stir in soynut butter. Using a fork, work in enough soy protein isolate to form a soft smooth paste. Let stand 5 minutes. Shape into ¾-inch (2 cm) balls. Balls should be soft but will firm up as they set. Roll in cocoa powder, shredded coconut or ground nuts, if desired. Place in attractive paper candy cups.

makes about 24 truffles
preparation time: 20 minutes
can be frozen but are best when eaten fresh.

PER TRUFFLE: 39 calories, 2 g protein, 4 g carbohydrate, 2 g total fat (< .5 g sat fat, < .5 g mono fat, < .5 g poly fat), < .5 mg cholesterol, 1 RE vitamin A*, 4 mcg folate*, 4 mg calcium*, < .5 mg iron*, 35 mg potassium, 2 mg sodium

soynut brittle
non-dairy

LOW IN fat, rich in potassium and isoflavones, this is crunchy candy at its best! A great snack for kids and adults.

1 cup	granulated sugar	250 mL
¼ cup	golden corn syrup	60 mL
2 tbsp.	coarsely crushed roasted soynuts	30 mL
¼ cup	peanuts, or other nuts	60 mL
¼ cup	slivered almonds	60 mL
1 tbsp.	soynut butter	15 mL
1 tbsp.	butter or margarine	15 mL
1½ tsp.	baking soda	7 mL
2 tbsp.	sliced or slivered almonds, as a topping	30 mL

- Grease a cookie sheet or line it with parchment paper.
- In a medium stainless steel saucepan, over medium heat, heat sugar with corn syrup stirring constantly until mixture is smooth and light golden in color. Stir in nuts, soynut butter, and butter; then stir in baking soda.
- While still foamy, pour hot mixture onto prepared cookie sheet and spread thinly. Immediately sprinkle with almonds. Cool completely on wire rack. Break into pieces.

makes about 1 lb. (450 g)
preparation and cooking time: 15 minutes

PER ½ OZ. (14 GRAMS): 54 calories, 1 g protein, 9 g carbohydrate, 2 g total fat (< .5 g sat fat, 1 g mono fat, < .5 g poly fat), 1 mg cholesterol, 1 g dietary fiber*, 3 RE vitamin A*, 3 mcg folate*, 6 mg calcium*, < .5 mg iron*, 21 mg potassium, 52 mg sodium

beverages

MY DAUGHTER Lara has concocted some delicious soy beverages that her university roommates have been eager to share with her. Creamy shakes or smoothies made with soy are not only nutritious but also flavorful. All you need is a blender to combine tofu, soy milk, and/or other soy foods with your favorite fruit(s), nuts, seeds, and flavorings. Following are a few tasty samples of this satisfying drink. All take just minutes to prepare.

banana daiquiri

ENJOY THIS refreshing drink with or without the rum. It's delicious either way.

2–4 oz.	dark rum	60–120 mL
1 tbsp.	honey	15 mL
2 tbsp.	fresh lime juice	30 mL
½ cup	vanilla soy milk	125 mL
2	ripe bananas, peeled and sliced	2
4–6	ice cubes	4–6

- In a blender, combine all ingredients until smooth. Pour into 2 tall glasses and serve immediately.

makes 2 servings
preparation time: 10 minutes

PER SERVING: 163 calories, 3 g protein, 38 g carbohydrate, 2 g total fat (< .5 g sat fat, < .5 g mono fat, 1 g poly fat), 4 g dietary fiber, 11 RE vitamin A, 25 mcg folate, 15 mg vitamin C, 11 mg calcium, 1 mg iron, 570 mg potassium, 9 mg sodium

banana soynut shake

2	medium ripe bananas	2
2 tbsp.	ground soynuts	30 mL
1/2 cup	soft tofu	125 mL
1 cup	vanilla soy milk	250 mL
1 tbsp.	sugar or honey, optional	15 mL
2–4	ice cubes	2–4

- Blend all ingredients in a blender until smooth.

makes about 2 cups (500 mL), or 2 servings

PER SERVING: 188 calories, 8 g protein, 32 g carbohydrate, 5 g total fat (< .5 g sat fat, < .5 g mono fat, 1 g poly fat), 5 g dietary fiber, 19 RE vitamin A, 24 mcg folate, 11 mg vitamin C, 34 mg calcium, 2 mg iron, 765 mg potassium, 24 mg sodium

coconut lychee banana shake

2 tbsp.	unsweetened shredded coconut	30 mL
6–8 (about ¹/₂ cup)	fresh or canned lychee nuts	6–8
1	ripe banana	1
1¹/₄ cup	vanilla soy milk	310 mL
2–4	ice cubes	2–4

• Blend all ingredients in a blender until smooth.

makes about 2 cups (500 mL), or 2 servings

cranberry **buttermilk** shake

½ cup	cranberry juice	125 mL
½ cup	buttermilk	125 mL
½ cup	soft tofu	125 mL
¼ cup	dried cranberries	60 mL
2 tbsp.	soy protein isolate, optional	30 mL
1–2 tbsp.	sugar or honey	15–30 mL
2–4	ice cubes	2–4

- Blend all ingredients in a blender until smooth.

**makes about 2 cups (500 mL),
or 2 servings**

PER SERVING: 156 calories, 6 g protein, 29 g carbohydrate, 3 g total fat ($<$ .5 g sat fat, $<$ .5 g mono fat, $<$ .5 g poly fat), 5 g dietary fiber, 11 RE vitamin A, 2 mcg folate, 14 mg vitamin C, 33 mg calcium, 1 mg iron, 219 mg potassium, 76 mg sodium

cranberry peach smoothie

3	ripe peaches, peeled and sliced	3
¼ cup	cranberry juice	60 mL
6 oz.	(1 container) vanilla soy yogurt	175 mL
½ cup	soft tofu	125 mL
2–4	ice cubes	2–4

• Blend all ingredients in a blender until smooth.

makes about 2 cups (500 mL),
 or 2 servings

PER SERVING: 178 calories, 7 g protein, 31 g carbohydrate, 3 g total fat (< .5 g sat fat, < .5 g mono fat, < .5 g poly fat), 4 g dietary fiber, 86 RE vitamin A, 5 mcg folate, 10 mg vitamin C, 41 mg calcium, 2 mg iron, 425 mg potassium, 30 mg sodium

protein berry shake
non-dairy

½ cup	soft tofu	125 mL
½ cup	soy milk	125 mL
¾ cup	fresh or frozen berries	175 mL
¼ cup	orange juice	60 mL
2 tbsp.	soy protein isolate	30 mL
2–4	ice cubes	2–4

• Blend all ingredients in a blender until smooth.

**makes about 2 cups (500 mL),
or 2 servings**

PER SERVING: 186 calories, 6 g protein, 31 g carbohydrate, 4 g total fat (1 g sat fat, < .5 g mono fat, 1 g poly fat), 3 g dietary fiber, 26 RE vitamin A, 8 mcg folate, 33 mg vitamin C, 27 mg calcium, 1 mg iron, 279 mg potassium, 12 mg sodium

raspberry kiwi shake

3	kiwis, peeled and quartered	3
½ cup	raspberries	125 mL
6 oz.	(1 container) vanilla soy yogurt	175 mL
½ cup	soft tofu	125 mL
1–2 tbsp.	maple syrup	15–30 mL
2–4	ice cubes, optional	2–4

- Blend all ingredients in a blender until smooth.

makes about 2 cups (500 mL), or 2 servings

PER SERVING: 218 calories, 8 g protein, 40 g carbohydrate, 4 g total fat (< .5 g sat fat, < .5 g mono fat, < .5 g poly fat), 7 g dietary fiber, 31 RE vitamin A, 51 mcg folate, 119 mg vitamin C, 74 mg calcium, 2 mg iron, 571 mg potassium, 33 mg sodium

orange strawberry smoothie
non-dairy

1 cup	orange juice	250 mL
6 oz.	(1 container) strawberry soy yogurt	175 mL
½ cup	frozen orange sherbet	125 mL
2–4	ice cubes	2–4

- Blend all ingredients in a blender until smooth.

**makes about 2 cups (500 mL),
or 2 servings**

VARIATIONS: Use plain soy yogurt and add 4–6 strawberries to the above ingredients before blending.

PER SERVING: 220 calories, 5 g protein, 45 g carbohydrate, 2 g total fat (1 g sat fat, < .5 g mono fat, < .5 g poly fat), 9 mg cholesterol, < .5 g dietary fiber, 10 RE vitamin A, 23 mcg folate, 41 mg vitamin C, 15 mg calcium, < .5 mg iron, 383 mg potassium, 69 mg sodium

peach almond shake

¹⁄₂ cup	soft tofu	125 mL
¹⁄₂ cup	vanilla soy milk	125 mL
4	ripe peaches, peeled and sliced	4
1 tbsp.	ground almonds	15 mL
	sugar or honey, to taste	
2–4	ice cubes	2–4

- Blend all ingredients in a blender until smooth.

**makes about 2 cups (500 mL),
or 2 servings**

PER SERVING: 159 calories, 7 g protein, 25 g carbohydrate, 5 g total fat (< .5 g sat fat, 1 g mono fat, 1 g poly fat), 6 g dietary fiber, 114 RE vitamin A, 8 mcg folate, 13 mg vitamin C, 40 mg calcium, 1 mg iron, 619 mg potassium, 12 mg sodium

mango flax seed shake

½ cup	soft tofu	125 mL
½ cup	vanilla soy milk	125 mL
1	ripe mango, peeled and chopped	1
1 tbsp.	frozen orange juice concentrate	15 mL
1 tbsp.	ground flax seed	15 mL
1 tbsp.	maple syrup	15 mL
2–4	ice cubes	2–4

- Blend all ingredients in a blender until smooth.

**makes about 2 cups (500 mL),
or 2 servings**

PER SERVING: 184 calories, 7 g protein, 30 g carbohydrate, 6 g total fat ($<$ .5 g sat fat, 1 g mono fat, 2 g poly fat), 5 g dietary fiber, 411 RE vitamin A, 34 mcg folate, 31 mg vitamin C, 53 mg calcium, 2 mg iron, 449 mg potassium, 17 mg sodium

caramel and amaretto hot chocolate

IS THERE any yummier drink on a cold day than a large steaming mug of hot chocolate? This is a delectable alternative to traditional hot chocolate. For a non-alcoholic drink leave out the Amaretto.

1 cup	chocolate soy milk	250 mL
¹/₂ oz.	semi-sweet chocolate, chopped, optional	14 g
1–2 tbsp.	Amaretto	15–30 mL
1–2 tbsp.	whipped cream	15–30 mL
1 tbsp.	Caramel Sauce, page 172	15 mL

- Over medium heat, or in microwave oven, bring chocolate soy milk to a boil. Stir in chocolate, if using, and Amaretto. Pour into a large mug. Top with whipped cream; drizzle with caramel sauce.

makes 1 large serving
preparation and cooking time: hot chocolate,
5 minutes, caramel sauce, 10 minutes

PER SERVING (ALCOHOLIC): 329 calories, 10 g protein, 39 g carbohydrate, 13 g total fat (2 g sat fat, 2 g mono fat, 2 g poly fat), 10 mg cholesterol, 3 g dietary fiber, 39 RE vitamin A, 4 mcg folate, < .5 mg vitamin C, 26 mg calcium, 2 mg iron, 404 mg potassium, 45 mg sodium

PER SERVING (NON-ALCOHOLIC): 270 calories, 10 g protein, 31 g carbohydrate, 13 g total fat (2 g sat fat, 2 g mono fat, 2 g poly fat), 10 mg cholesterol, 3 g dietary fiber, 39 RE vitamin A, 4 mcg folate, < .5 mg vitamin C, 26 mg calcium, 2 mg iron, 399 mg potassium, 44 mg sodium

holiday eggnog
non-dairy

HOW ABOUT a glass of eggnog to get you, your family and friends into the holiday spirit?

1 cup	vanilla soy milk	250 mL
1 cup	liquid eggs	250 mL
2 tbsp.	confectioner's sugar	30 mL
2–3 tbsp.	brandy (optional)	30–45 mL
	grated nutmeg, as a garnish	

- Combine first 4 ingredients in a blender. Process until smooth and frothy. Pour into glasses and sprinkle with nutmeg. Serve immediately.

**makes about 2 cups,
or 3 servings**

VARIATIONS: For a richer and creamier version, blend Basic Vanilla Sauce, page 171, into this eggnog.

PER SERVING: 134 calories, 14 g protein, 10 g carbohydrate, 5 g total fat ($<$.5 g sat fat, $<$.5 g mono fat, 1 g poly fat), 1 g dietary fiber, 2 RE vitamin A, 1 mcg folate, 3 mg calcium, $<$.5 mg iron, 117 mg potassium, 177 mg sodium

I WOULD like to thank the following people for their invaluable help, support, and encouragement: my daughter Bettina Allen, for her enthusiastic dedication to this project which resulted in her contribution of several recipes as well as the nutritional analysis for all of the recipes in this book; Bev Jong, whose organizational skills enabled me to submit an orderly manuscript to my publisher in record time; my family, friends, and neighbors, whose appreciation for healthy sweets qualified them as excellent taste testers and critics.

index